# BUILDING YOUR LADDER

# BUILDING YOUR LADDER

## An Associate's Guide to Success Beyond Partnership

MARIAN LEE

Printed in the United States of America.

16 15 14 13 12   5 4 3 2 1

Library of Congress Cataloging-in-Publication Data on file.

ISBN 978-1-61438-904-0

Discounts are available for books ordered in bulk. Special consideration is given to state bars, CLE programs, and other bar-related organizations. Inquire at Book Publishing, ABA Publishing, American Bar Association, 321 North Clark Street, Chicago, Illinois 60654-7598.

www.ShopABA.org

# Contents

Chapter 6
**Continually Improve Your Product**

Chapter 7
**Remember That Relationships Are Everything**

Chapter 8
**Distinguish Yourself: What Makes You So Special?**

# Acknowledgments

It's dangerous to name names when giving thanks and credit, because you will inevitably forget someone you should have included. So at the outset, I express a collective "thank you" to all of the highly talented lawyers I've been fortunate to have worked with during my career. I'm also grateful to all of the clients I worked with, who continually pulled me away from the theoretical aspects of law and forced me to focus on the practical. I want to thank my colleagues in the Denver and Colorado Bar Associations, who shared with me valuable practice tips, volunteer projects, their friendship, and many enjoyable cocktail hours. And my colleagues in the Professional Development Consortium, who unselfishly share their wisdom and experience. Things I learned from all of these people are found throughout this book.

Specifically, however, I need to mention those who most directly enabled me to write this book:

I was blessed to have had some incredible mentors along my journey, a group of preeminent lawyers who helped me feel like I belonged in this profession. Some of them provided input specifically for this book, while others taught me lessons at some point that indirectly found expression here: Jack Deisch, who saw in me as a law clerk the potential to become a successful lawyer, and encouraged me when I doubted I could; David Zisser, a lawyer with razor-sharp intellect who didn't let me get away with anything, even as a new associate; Ken Skogg, my friend, mentor, role model, and advisor, who directed opportunities to me, gave me work when I needed it most, and provided invaluable insights that are woven into most of the themes in this book; Hugh Gottschalk, who shared with me his passion for practicing law, and his ability to cut to the chase of any situation with uncanny accuracy; Dave Stark, who consistently took the high road and taught me to do the same; Terence Ridley, my mentor and friend, who gave me praise and encouragement but kicked my butt when I needed it; and finally, Miles Cortez, my former partner and mentor, and current sage and friend.

I also want to the thank senior associates at my firm who shared their wisdom and spot-on advice with me. At one point during the writing of this book, I became stuck. I had some material, but not enough, and didn't know quite how to frame what I had. These talented associates provided a fresh perspective that only those who are in the transitioning-to-partner trenches now—as opposed to 16 years ago, when I was—can provide. They rescued me by providing great quotes and helped me focus on some important points: Geoff Williamson, Kristin Macdonald, Cristal Deherrera, Josh Hantman, Jonathan Sandier, Amy Steinfeld and Jonathan Pray. In the time since they provided their input, Josh, Amy, and Jonathan have become partners, a role in which I'm certain all three will thrive.

Additionally, several of my friends and colleagues provided input for this book, as well as encouragement and support: Bob Bricmont, who at various times played the roles of my law review colleague, landlord, lawyer, friend and advisor; Phil Gosch, a partner at my firm who provided valuable insights about associate success; Steve Hensen, who loves and respects the practice of law more than anyone I know; Carolynne White, my close friend who provided input, encouragement and support; and especially, Joni Burleson, who has pursued both the practice of law and leadership in the community with a passion the rest of us can only emulate. Joni provided me with input, editing, inspiration, and accountability for getting this book written.

I received tremendous support and assistance from my non-lawyer friends as well. There are two groups in particular I'd like to acknowledge. First, a group of women I met twelve years ago, when I was at a pivotal point in my career. These women inspired me and emboldened me to embark on a path toward developing others: Barb Simasko, Vickie Thomas, Sandy Dixon, and Anne Prather. Second, I received encouragement from a group of professionals who, like me, are driven to coach and inspire others: Bill Lindberg, Greg Reinhart, Jane Gietzen, Hien DeYoung, MaryAnn Anderson, Susan Azavedo, and Scott Weisberg. At a coaching program we all attended, they helped me overcome many of the internal obstacles that threatened to keep me from writing this book. And special thanks to Greg, who as part of his own coaching certification training, coached me and kept me on track to write this book.

My thanks would not be complete without mentioning my publishing friends: Merrilyn Tarlton, a law practice management expert and gifted writer and editor who has advised me, encouraged me, and published my work. Greg Smith, the first person who confirmed the possibility that I could write this book; and Tim Brandhorst, who believed in my concept for this book and ultimately made it happen.

Finally, I must thank those who define my everyday existence. My mother, who loves books and planted in me the burning desire to write one someday; my brother, Bret, who inspires me every day with his courage; and my children, Amber and Sean, who've provided me with both a reason for my career and refuge from it. Their presence in my life has been a gift and one of the greatest learning experiences of all, always helping me remember what matters most in life.

# About the Author

**Marian Lee** has been immersed in the legal profession for over 26 years, having learned the practice of law, lawyer recruiting and development, and law practice management from a wide array of vantage points. As a full-time clerk for two years during law school, an associate and later counsel in local and national law firms, a sole practitioner, a founding partner of a litigation boutique, and a lawyer development consultant. She writes and speaks on topics related to success as a lawyer, the track to partnership, career development, and lawyer training and mentoring. She is currently the Director of Professional Development and Risk Management at Brownstein Hyatt Farber Schreck, LLP, a 230-attorney firm based in Denver.

# The Realities of Today's Legal Economy

This book is for lawyers who want to excel in the private practice of law. Whether you are an associate who wants to become a successful partner someday, a partner who wants to become more valuable to a firm, or a sole practitioner who wants to take your practice to the next level, the advice in this book can advance your career.

Once upon a time, you could do solid work as an associate, achieve some notable successes, bill a respectable number of hours, and reasonably expect to make partner in five to seven years. Once you made partner, you had relative job security and could develop your practice at a comfortable pace. You had several years to ramp up, learn the skills necessary to build a practice, and add value as a co-owner of the firm. Your partners would be patient with you and would not expect too much right away. Over time, you would try to build your book of business; but if you didn't, the firm could still make room for you. Your compensation would likely be affected, but in most cases your position was secure.

Those days are over. Grappling with the market downturn, a fragile economy, reduced demand for legal services, and tighter client control over legal spending, law firms are promoting fewer associates to partnership and looking more closely at the performance of existing partners, particularly in the junior ranks. In firms that have two-tiered partnership structures, nonequity partners face greater difficulty transitioning to equity status than they did five years ago. In firms without two-tier structures, new partners are nonetheless under pressure to establish themselves and reassure their firms that they have what it takes to succeed in the long term.

As a new partner in today's legal world, you can no longer ramp up at a leisurely pace. In a relatively short time, you need to prove that you can produce and manage business, manage people, and add value to the firm in other ways as well. If you can't do all of that quickly, ideally within two to four years of becoming a partner, you become vulnerable to stagnation, reduced internal referrals, and, ultimately, shown the door. When economic times are hard, nonequity partners can become prime targets because they are more highly paid than associates but don't produce business like equity partners.

Unlike the old days, a new partner can no longer rest on his laurels and assume that he has "made it." To the contrary, a new development phase is just beginning, one in which the work will get harder, the expectations will be higher, and the pressure will feel greater. In fact, the initial attainment of partnership has been characterized as only the fourth stage in a nine-stage career progression.[1] There are new sets of challenges ahead in order to clear the second partnership hurdle and attain the ownership benefits and relative job security that attend the status of an equity partner.

Meeting these new challenges will require skills and talents you didn't necessarily need in order to succeed as an associate. Although experiences vary widely from firm to firm and from practice to practice, most associates aren't expected to develop significant business, achieve prominent status in their practice area, assume primary client management, take a firm leadership role, or manage subordinates to a great extent. For the most part, they are only expected to produce solid work, be good team players, show loyalty to the firm, and be dependable.

Despite the significant differences in expectations, most firms provide surprisingly little guidance to associates about the skills they will need to succeed as partners. Imagine the jolt that many new partners feel

---

[1] MARK I. SIRKIN, FROM 3L TO 401(K): SEASONS OF AN ATTORNEY'S LIFE 3 (West LegalEdcenter 2010) (white paper). According to Sirkin, the nine stages are as follows: (1) summer/early associate, (2) midlevel associate, (3) prepartner associate, (4) early partner, (5) midlevel partner, (6) practice leader, (7) division leader, (8) management committee member, and (9) managing partner. *Id.*

when, after recovering from the giddiness surrounding their first major promotion, they realize that their firms have not prepared them to meet the new demands they are suddenly making of them.

Because partner-level skills take years to develop, it's critical that as an associate, you look ahead to your ultimate goals. If owning your own practice and having control over your career are among those goals, the sooner you start preparing, the better off you will be. Although it's important for a new lawyer to focus in the first two or three years on becoming an excellent lawyer, once the basics have been mastered, it's time to look ahead.

### What This Book Is Not

Different firms have different cultures, values, and priorities. Fundamentally, however, they all need the same kinds of contributions from their partners in order to sustain themselves: legal talent, business development, client service, management, and leadership. Nonetheless, this is not a book about how to make partner. Although developing partner-level skills may well increase your chances of promotion, this book assumes that you don't just want to arrive at partnership but that you want to thrive there. Nor does this book purport to guarantee long-term success in a given firm without regard to the general state of the economy, the financial health of the firm, or the relative demand for lawyers in the associate's particular practice area.

Secondly, this book does not purport to have all the answers; rather, it is intended to alert you to the questions you should be asking, the experience you should be seeking, and the skills you should be learning if you want to be successful as a partner. It contains references to a number of excellent materials for delving further into any particular topic. It is intended to raise awareness and provide basic advice; it will be up to you to implement this advice, seek out the resources you need, and plan your development accordingly. Each attorney has his own strengths and talents and makes his own mix of contributions to a firm. It's essential to assess yourself and what you have to offer, decide where you need to grow, and prepare to contribute in a variety of ways. The more you contribute, the more valuable you will be to your firm and the more rewarding your career will be.

### Other Choices

This book is also not intended to suggest that the only desirable career path is to become a partner in a law firm. Many lawyers find satisfaction in solo practice, government agencies, in-house positions, contract attorney work, and myriad other nontraditional career paths. Indeed, before you launch yourself on any career path, and every few years while you are on it, you need to take stock of your goals. You need to ask yourself whether the work you are doing and the place in which you're doing it are moving you toward your long-term goals for both your career and your personal life. If your day-to-day practice is not in harmony with your ultimate objectives and highest values, no amount of coaching or development will make you happy with what you are doing.

### Industry Trends Affecting Legal Careers

The drastic changes that have occurred in the legal market over the past five years have both limiting and potentially advantageous implications.[2] The makeup of law firms is changing from the traditional model in which the vast majority of lawyers are partnership-track associates, a small percentage are "counsel" or nonpartnership senior lawyers, and there is a cadre of partners to a model in which the number of partnership-track associates is decreased significantly and there are many more nontraditional categories of experienced lawyers, a significant layer of income partners, and a small band of equity partners. You may well choose a nonpartnership or reduced-hour track to serve your personal goals and find great satisfaction in doing so.

The composition of the equity partner ranks is changing as well. Although traditionally the majority of law firm partners came up

---

[2] James W. Jones, Senior Fellow, Ctr. for the Study of the Legal Profession, Georgetown Univ. Law Cent., Plenary Address at the Nat'l Ass'n for Legal Career Prof'ls (NALP) Conference 2012: Understanding the Current Legal Economy (Apr. 20, 2012).

through internal promotion, there has been a shift among firms over the past years toward lateral acquisitions as a means of expanding their equity partner ranks.[3] That trend has both positive and negative aspects. On the negative side, senior associates and income partners now face increased competition from lawyers outside the firm for eventual equity partner positions. On the plus side, however, there are an increasing number of alternative career paths available to lawyers in general. Firms are more focused on substantive expertise in specific practice areas. Thus, an early career choice to work in a government or in-house position doesn't necessarily preclude you from changing gears later and becoming an attractive lateral partner candidate. In fact, the subject matter expertise you gained may make you even more marketable.

Another trend is outsourcing. Both clients and law firms are increasingly turning to lower-cost solutions for basic legal services such as document review, due diligence, drafting, and brief writing. There are two sets of implications to this trend. On the one hand, it opens a nontraditional career path for those who want to work from home or more flexibly on a contract basis and are satisfied with doing a narrow scope of work. On the other hand, it creates some pressure but provides greater incentive for developing yourself into someone who can run a law practice from soup to nuts. Competent technicians can be outsourced, but attorneys who can run a law practice cannot. One of the greatest sources of anxiety for many associates is their perception that they are viewed by their firms as "fungible goods" that can be easily replaced. That can become a self-fulfilling prophecy for associates who offer only solid legal skills. The best insurance against fungibility is to demonstrate your potential to also attract and retain clients, manage your work in a profitable manner, and lead effective teams.

Another trend is that the number of years to initial partnership eligibility is increasing, on average, from a seven- to eight-year track ten years ago to a ten- to twelve-year track today, particularly in larger firms. This is not necessarily a bad thing if you take advantage of those addi-

---

[3] HILDEBRANDT INST., 2012 CLIENT ADVISORY 14 (2012).

tional years to start performing like a partner. It's much better to fully develop yourself, make partner at year ten, and be well on your way to equity partnership status than to make partner at year seven, fail to ramp up within three to four years, and become a sideline player.

The fact that firms are making fewer equity partners means, inevitably, that the process is more competitive. You may not rise to partner in your firm; instead, you may change firms or choose another career path altogether. But no matter what path you choose, you will be more marketable and have more options if you've developed the full range of management, relationship-building, and communication skills discussed in this book.

If you want to achieve success as a partner—the freedom to direct your own career and make your own choices rather than having them limited by others—the sooner you start preparing for your new role, the better off you'll be. In today's legal environment where entire practice groups change firms, firms alter the careers of their lawyers by merging with one another, firms dissolve when they can no longer stay competitive, and layoffs occur when economic times get hard, "career development and the pursuit of marketability must be an ongoing personal priority."[4]

---

[4] JUDITH N. COLLINS, PAULA A. PATTON & ABBIE F. WILLARD, THE LATERAL LAWYER: WHY THEY LEAVE AND WHAT MAY MAKE THEM STAY 9 (NALP Found. for Research & Educ. 2001).

# CHAPTER ONE

# Think Ahead: What Got You Here Won't Necessarily Get You There

*In a field one summer's day a Grasshopper was hopping about, chirp-ing and singing to its heart's content. An Ant passed by, bearing along with great toil an ear of corn he was taking to the nest.*

*"Why not come and chat with me," said the Grasshopper, "instead of toiling and moiling in that way?"*

*"I am helping to lay up food for the winter," said the Ant, "and rec-ommend you to do the same."*

*"Why bother about winter?" said the Grasshopper; ["]we have got plenty of food at present." But the Ant went on its way and continued its toil. When the winter came the Grasshopper had no food and found itself dying of hunger, while it saw the ants distributing every day corn and grain from the stores they had collected in the summer. Then the Grasshopper knew:*

*It is best to prepare for the days of necessity.*

*—Aesop[1]*

When you're an associate receiving positive feedback for your intel-ligence, diligence, and impeccable work product, it's hard to fathom the need to start learning an entirely different set of skills for the later phases

---

[1] Aesop, *The Ant and the Grasshopper, in* AESOP'S FABLES, http://www.aesopfables.com/cgi/aesop1.cgi?sel& TheAntandtheGrasshopper&&antgrass.ram (last visited Nov. 9, 2012).

of your career. But success as an associate does not guarantee long-term success as a partner. It's a mistake to assume that if you are made a partner, you necessarily have all the skills, knowledge, and behaviors you need in order to prosper in the long term. Unfortunately, most law firms don't do much to prepare their associates for their eventual role as partners; rather, they encourage and evaluate associates on the skills and attributes that make them valuable in supporting roles, primarily legal skills. Over time and in the right environment, associates may learn some business and interpersonal skills, but this typically occurs on a hit-or-miss basis unless they actively seek to develop such skills.

Although your status increases and there may be some pay (and billing rate) increase associated with becoming a partner, this increase is bestowed upon you not so much because you are suddenly more valuable to the firm, but rather because the firm is investing in you and betting that you will grow into your new role. The promotion to partner is much more a forward-looking decision—a leap of faith based on what the firm thinks you can contribute as a partner—rather than a backward-looking decision to reward you for being a good associate. This is an important distinction to recognize because you will remain relatively vulnerable until you fulfill your perceived potential.

The trap into which some new partners fall is viewing the promotion as a reward for past performance, believing that they have "made it" and either not focusing on developing or starting too late to develop the skills necessary to make the new contributions that partners are expected to make in exchange for increased status, more compensation, and an ownership interest in the firm. Young partners who don't live up to the firm's expectations to lose ground in their careers, can stagnate, and essentially become overpaid associates. It can only benefit your career to start learning how to add value as a partner as soon as possible.

### The Five Critical Skill Sets

To practice successfully as a partner in a law firm, you'll need strength in several groups of skills: legal skills, business development, client relations, practice management, and leadership. Although different firms and practice groups use their associates differently, it's not unheard of for associates make it all the way to partnership based entirely on their legal ability. These associates are often surprised to arrive at partnership and find out that they should have been working on the other four skill sets as well, whether or not the firm or the partners they worked for actually told them to do so.

Although no partner will be equally strong in all five areas, the more diverse your range of skills, the better your long-term outlook. With few exceptions, lawyers must have more than legal skills to sustain a successful career. Those exceptions will become even rarer if current trends continue as the increasingly competitive legal economy requires lawyers to maintain a constant focus on business development, pay meticulous attention to client relationships, manage their work diligently, and reinvent their practices to stay profitable.

## Legal Skills

The first of the five skill sets is the most obvious and the one on which most associates focus the majority of their efforts. To be successful as a partner, an attorney must achieve a degree of professional stature and earn a reputation for diligence, competence, and solid results for clients. The fundamental skills that build this kind of stature are a continuously expanding knowledge of the substantive law in a particular practice area, sound judgment, analytical skills, and the ability to communicate cogently and persuasively both orally and in writing.

In 2007, the Carnegie Foundation released *Educating Lawyers: Preparation for the Profession of Law*, a report that examined the skills and attributes necessary to practice law successfully and recommended modifications to traditional law school education to help foster those qualities in students. Noting that historically law school education separated knowledge (the substance of law), skills (the "how," or practical side), and ethics (the "why"), the Carnegie report identified three "apprenticeships" that are essential components of legal education: (1)

intellectual or cognitive component; (2) practice-based/performance skills; and (3) identity and purpose.[2] The report suggested that the purely analytical framework imposed on students from their first year, which promotes legal problem solving, actually dehumanizes the practitioners and participants.[3] The authors further suggested that law school removes the ethical, social, and moral roots of law while stripping the lawyer and client of professional and personal identity.[4]

The authors of the Carnegie report observed that legal education has traditionally overvalued the importance of the first apprenticeship—the intellectual side—and undervalued the second two.[5] The intellectual and cognitive apprenticeship may be analogized to the legal skill set described in this book, and the other skill sets relate generally to the second two apprenticeships as practical and people skills.

The Carnegie authors expressed concern that to the extent that the nonlegal apprenticeship skills are being taught in law school at all, they are not well integrated with intellectual or cognitive components.[6] They also noted that the very method by which law is taught, i.e., the Socratic method, has focused on the intellectual component. This focus is further illustrated by the fact that law students are generally taught to learn legal principles in the objective, impersonal context of *cases* rather than the personal, subjective context of *clients*. The report concluded by calling for a greater emphasis on the formation of professional identity along with teaching theory and practice.[7]

Because traditionally law schools have focused almost exclusively on legal principles, reasoning, and analysis, it has historically fallen to experienced practitioners to teach new lawyers the practical and people-related skills necessary to succeed as a lawyer. As firms have grown larger and billable-hour pressures greater, however, senior lawyers have more difficulty finding the time and incentive to train junior lawyers exten-

---

[2] WILLIAM M. SULLIVAN ET AL., CARNEGIE FOUND., EDUCATING LAWYERS: PREPARATION FOR THE PROFESSION OF LAW 79 (Jossey-Bass 2007).

[3] *Id.*

[4] *Id.*

[5] *Id.*

[6] *Id.* at 59.

[7] *Id.* at 13.

sively. Much has been written about the less personal process of training lawyers today and the need for firms to implement structures to help ensure that new lawyers receive the training and mentoring they need. The impact of this learning gap is apparent in junior partners who received enough training and experience in the intellectual aspects of law practice to become productive associates and eventually make partner, but did not receive enough training in the practice and people-oriented aspects to sustain their careers in the long run. "It isn't enough to be a good lawyer; the job is to make money for the firm."[8]

## Business Development

This category encompasses a variety of skills and activities such as networking, branding yourself, developing a niche, self-promotion, client consciousness, and the ability to recognize and seize opportunities. It requires a hungry, entrepreneurial spirit. These skills and abilities are the ones most often ignored in associates. Ironically, a lack of these skills is often the most frequent reason for lack of success as a partner.

Many firms are schizophrenic with their associates with regard to rainmaking, telling them in the early years that they do not want them to focus on bringing in business, but later judging them harshly when they arrive at the threshold of partnership without having developed the foundational skills necessary for effective business development. Although associates are generally limited in their ability to produce significant clients, they should be spending their prepartnership years building a platform—a network, an awareness of the potential client market, and some visibility—that will enable them to develop business later on.

## Client Relations

It's one thing to bring in a new client. It's another thing to maintain and grow the relationship. Some lawyers who excel at rainmaking do not possess the same level of skill at maintaining and growing clients after

---

[8] Jennifer Smith, "Law-Firm Partners Face Layoffs," WALL ST J., Jan. 6, 2013. *See also* 2013 Client Advisory by Hildebrandt Consulting LLC at 33 (noting increase in number of income partners but decrease in productivity).

they come in the door. And many lawyers who excel at client relations are not necessarily great rainmakers. While risk taking, entrepreneurial spirit, and creativity are the hallmarks of a great rainmaker, sensitivity, great communication skills, and adaptability are the strengths of lawyers who excel at client relations.

Lawyers who excel at client relations keep their clients apprised of what's going on in their matters. They pick up the phone when there's an important development or decision to be made and call the client. They manage expectations so that the client has a realistic view of the likely outcome of the representation. Most of all, great client keepers are great listeners, a rare attribute among attorneys who are eager to show clients how much they know. Associates who are fortunate enough to get significant client contact can flourish in this role and take advantage of the opportunity to learn these skills.

## Practice Management

You can have clients and be a good lawyer, but if you don't manage your practice well, you are likely to create ethical and financial problems for yourself. Management skills include understanding what makes a firm profitable, allocating your time wisely, recording your time diligently, reviewing your pro forma statements and prebills in a timely and thorough manner, and letting go of unprofitable work and clients. Many associates receive little or no exposure to this skill set other than learning to bill time and juggle multiple projects at once.

## Leadership

The leadership skill set referenced throughout this book encompasses a blend of qualities that involve looking beyond one's self. This includes the ability to develop the talent in others; serve the organization as a whole; inspire, encourage, and persuade others, set and reach goals, and influence others to serve the firm's interests. These skills are often overlooked in associate evaluations, and associates can make partner having very few of them.

Because the majority of leadership positions within a firm are given to partners rather than associates, a good way for associates to develop these skills is to look outside the firm. By joining volunteer or community organizations, associates can find opportunities to learn about particular community issues, expand their network, and eventually serve in a leadership role. Leading a committee or board for a small nonprofit organization provides great practice for leading teams and committees within your firm later on. Other sources of early leadership opportunities may include the Young Lawyers Division of your local or state bar association.

### Attitudes

Although developing skills in all five skill sets can set you on a path to success, pervading all of these skills and activities is the need to maintain a positive attitude. "Stay positive" is a clichéd piece of advice, yet universal in its validity.

One of the most fundamental revelations that occurs to a new partner is that his livelihood will now depend, to a great extent, on how he impacts the people around him. Although an associate can, theoretically, spend eight years producing great work product on his own, moving to the next level means influencing others—influencing clients to hire you, associates and staff to do great work for you, and others in the firm to serve the group's collective best interests.

In order to influence others, you need a positive attitude. You need to exude confidence and see the best in people and give them the benefit of the doubt. You need to be curious, realizing that there is always more to learn and that you can learn something of value from every person you meet.

### Relationships

Another common attribute of a successful lawyer is a predisposition toward building relationships. You can't be a successful partner alone: you need other people. And the ability to influence these people depends largely on the kinds of relationships you build—at home, in the community, with your friends, within your firm, and within the profession. David Maister said it best: "Logic and rationality will only take you so far; the most important thing you can learn is how to interact with other people. Everything you'll want in professional life (and outside it) will come from another person: a client, a colleague, a superior or a subordinate."[9]

As discussed more fully in later chapters, the ability to build and maintain relationships is critical to a successful career and often makes the difference between stagnating after a promising run as an associate and thriving as a partner in the long term.

### *The Ability to Add Value Gets You Marketability, Rewards, and Freedom*

Everyone brings a unique set of skills, knowledge, and talents to the profession. Your formula for success will be different from that of your colleague. Regardless of what you bring to the table, strive to continue developing the full package of legal, business, and interpersonal skills throughout your career.

The irony is that the more skills you develop and thus the more valuable you are to your firm, the more job security and freedom you will have. Because you'll be more attractive and marketable to other firms, your current firm will likely want to keep you by giving you fair compensation and ample resources to help you build your practice. If it doesn't, you have the freedom to leave. In short, the more marketable you are, the more choices you have and the more control you'll have over your career.

---

[9] DAVID H. MAISTER, ADVICE TO A YOUNG PROFESSIONAL 1 (2005), *available at* davidmaister.com/pdf/Some AdvicetoaYoungProfessional20912.pdf.

CHAPTER TWO

# Understand the Business
# You Want to Own Someday:
# A Primer on Law Firm Economics

*The Blind Men and the Elephant*

*A group of blind men heard that a strange animal, called an ele-
phant, had been brought to the town, but none of them were aware
of its shape and form. Out of curiosity, they said: "We must inspect
and know it by touch, of which we are capable." So, they sought it
out, and when they found it they groped about it. In the case of the
first person, whose hand landed on the trunk, said, "This being is
like a drain pipe." For another one whose hand reached its ear, it
seemed like a kind of fan. As for another person, whose hand was
upon its leg, said, "I perceive the shape of the elephant to be like a pil-
lar." And in the case of the one who placed his hand upon its back
said, "Indeed, this elephant is like a throne." Now, each of these presented a true aspect when he related what he had gained from expe-
riencing the elephant. None of them had strayed from the true
description of the elephant. Yet they fell short of fathoming the true
appearance of the elephant.*

Like the blind men who knew only isolated facts about the elephant,
many associates enter the practice with little awareness of the factors
that cause law firms to succeed or fail as businesses. From their limited
vantage point, inexperienced associates may overestimate their own
profitability and underestimate the variables that come between the

9

number of hours they bill and the actual revenue that the firm ultimately receives. Touching only a portion of the law firm "elephant," they may do the basic math by multiplying their annual billable hours by their hourly billing rate and then subtracting their salary and conclude that they are grossly underpaid. There is, however, much more to the story. In order to appreciate the associate's role in law firm profitability, as well as the value that an associate will be able to add as a partner someday, it's helpful to understand the basics of law firm economics.

### Generation of Revenue

In order to make money, law firms must generate revenue. The sole source of revenue for law firms is the services of their lawyers. However, there are several steps that must occur before a lawyer's work turns into revenue for the firm: the lawyer must do the work, the lawyer must keep track of the time spent on the work, the lawyer must enter the time into the firm's billing system, the firm must produce a supportable billing statement for the client, and the firm must receive payment from the client (i.e., the client must be willing and able to pay the bill).

### Doing the Work

Because law firms do not manufacture goods or store inventory, they depend on their lawyers to continually provide legal services for clients. When lawyers take vacations or leave of any kind, they are not generating revenue. In order to maintain a firm's profitability, a sufficient quantity of work must be produced on a continuous basis to keep the pipeline full and pay the overhead and salaries necessary to continue operating.

### Keeping Track of Time

Although alternative fees are gaining traction with some clients, most legal work is still done on an hourly-fee basis. Under this system, work is useless if the hours spent on client work are not recorded. Time that is not recorded is like inventory that is thrown in the trash and never available for sale.

### Entering Time

Even if the lawyer works and records his time, there is no potential benefit to the firm until that time is somehow entered into the firm's billing system, whether by the lawyer directly or by an administrative assistant. Time that is worked, and even tracked, is worth nothing if it never makes its way into the system that turns that time into receivable revenue.

### Producing a Supportable Billing Statement

Clients must have a bill in order to pay for the legal services they receive. However, generating a bill requires more than a computer print-out; it requires that the lawyer in charge of the client relationship review the time entries to make sure they are supportable. This includes an examination of how long it took to complete particular tasks, whether the appropriate personnel worked on the file, whether the work conformed to the fee agreement, and whether the work conformed to any billing guidelines that client may have imposed. In this process, time must sometimes be "written off" because it pertains to tasks for which the client is not likely to pay. Some potential fees are lost in this process, depending on the efficiency of the working attorney. The reviewing lawyer must also examine the way the various tasks are described. When attorneys are vague about the work they do, e.g., billing .4 hours for a generic "phone conference," a client may not see value in the time and may refuse to pay. Clients are more likely to pay if the attorney writes down a .4 hour entry for "telephone conference between J. Smith and F. Jones regarding potential defenses to assert in answer to complaint." In addition, the bill must reflect the rate agreed upon by the client. If the fee agreement included a discount, then the firm will not receive the full hourly rate for the work billed to the client.

### Receiving Payment for the Bill

After a client receives a bill, particularly if it is a large one, it will be carefully reviewed by the client, its accounting department, or sometimes an outside auditing firm. Clients look for reasons to save money and not to pay bills because they are under economic pressures just like everyone else. However, if the relationship attorney has done a good job of editing the bill before it goes out, there should be few problems.

But there are reasons why clients may refuse to pay a particular bill or to pay for certain services listed on a bill. These reasons may include the firm (a) failing to follow the client's billing guidelines, (b) taking too long on a particular task, (c) using too many different people on a particular matter (e.g., attorneys, paralegals, document clerks), or (d) charging for work that the client did not authorize. The client would then contact the firm and request that the bill be reduced. After this process, the amount ultimately paid may be further reduced.

In addition to clearing these hurdles, the work will not turn into cash unless the client is able to pay. Sometimes clients cannot afford a particular bill either because it was more than they expected or because their cash flow was less than expected. This can further interfere with the firm's anticipated cash flow.

### Management of Expenses

Once the revenue is generated, it must be used to pay the law firm's expenses. Expense ratios can vary from firm to firm, but generally salaries for nonpartner attorneys and staff account for the highest percentage of total expenses. Other significant expenses include rent and technology. Depending on the size of the firm, it is likely to incur some administrative costs, such as marketing, recruiting, training, charity, bar dues, retreats, and library expenses. If the firm uses debt to finance its operations, it will have debt service expense as well.

Associates often wonder how much profit their firm makes from the work they do. There are varying statistics about how long it takes for an associate to become profitable, but typical estimates range from one and a half to three years after a first-year associate is hired, and from six to eighteen months after a lateral associate is hired. This delay results from the fact that the firm incurs many up-front expenses in hiring the associate, including costs of recruiting, training, and writing off time on matters as the new associate gets "up to speed." These costs are incurred before the associate gets into a routine, creates a regular flow of work, and starts billing efficiently and the hours billed are eventually paid. Other up-front costs incurred for each new attorney include incremental costs for support staff, computers, phones, and attorney licenses and bar memberships. Furthermore, in addition to salary, the firm incurs costs for benefits, which can easily exceed $50,000 per year per lawyer, depending on the firm's overall benefit package.

### *Other Variables Affecting Profitability*

In addition to the degree to which a firm effectively controls expenses, its profitability is affected by other drivers as well.

## Productivity

Perhaps the most obvious driver of law firm profitability is the productivity of its lawyers. The more hours the lawyers bill, the more potential revenue the firm generates. For many years, most large firms focused on this driver more than any other, incentivizing associates to bill as many hours as they possibly could. The push for additional hours has traditionally been a popular way to increase revenue because the firm incurs virtually no additional incremental costs for the extra hours above the minimum. For example, if a firm's billable-hour expectation for associates is eighteen hundred hours, the firm budgets a certain amount of overhead cost for each associate to generate those hours, including office space, secretarial support, computers, etc. If an associate bills two thousand hours rather than eighteen hundred, the additional two hundred hours (as is true of every additional hour beyond the minimum) goes straight to the bottom line because there are typically little or no incremental costs associated with them.

The ability of firms to increase revenue by increasing billable hours has been limited since the economic downturn, however, as demand for legal services has dropped and institutional clients are demanding greater value and efficiency for their legal fee dollars. Clients are increasingly sensitive to preventing overbilling and padding of hours and more frequently requiring their outside counsel to adhere to strict budgets, particularly for predictable tasks.

In addition, many clients are requesting alternative fee arrangements that are not based on billable hours but rather on project tasks accomplished or results produced by the work. Although currently, alternative fee arrangements generate only about 13 percent of large law firm revenues,[1] this percentage is likely to grow in the future. The more common such arrangements become, the more law firms will have to rely on sound project management and efficient delivery as measures of productivity. As efficiency becomes a greater focus in providing legal services (similar to the way efficiency historically has been a focus in other industries), the concept of a lawyer spending more time than necessary on a given task will be viewed as a cost to be avoided rather than a revenue-generating activity to be encouraged.

## Leverage

A cornerstone of the law firm business model, leverage is the principle that a firm will be more profitable if a given partner who brings in business can keep a number of associates (or other nonpartner lawyers) busy with client work. It stands to reason that if a law firm's partners are the only ones doing the work they generate, their potential revenue will be limited by the number of hours the partner can work in a year. By passing work down to an associate, a partner can free up hours to bill and generate additional work and create more revenue from the work he brings in. It also means that more work is getting done by lawyers who will not share in the profits generated, so revenue grows without decreasing the size of each share of the pie.

In recent years, however, the leverage model has changed as firms have reduced their associate ranks through layoffs and reduced hiring levels. At the same time, the numbers of nonequity partners have increased, in some instances through "de-equitization" of former equity partners. As an alternative means of increasing leverage, firms have increased their use of contract and part-time lawyers, who offer a lower-

[1] Jennifer Smith, *Companies Reset Legal Costs*, WALL ST J., Apr. 8, 2012.

cost form of leverage than traditional associates. The effective use of paralegals can also increase leverage, especially in practices such as litigation, family law, and estate planning.

## Rates

The higher the billing rates a law firm can charge, the more revenue it can generate from a given number of billable hours. Rate increases can occur on an individual or firm-wide basis. Individually, a lawyer's rate may increase as his experience increases, as he develops a particular practice specialty, or as he gains an established reputation. On a firm-wide basis, prior to the recession, firms were raising rates at a rate of 6 percent to 8 percent per year. Partly as a result of these increases, the overall costs of legal services grew exponentially, far in excess of the rate of inflation. Ultimately, these "automatic" yearly increases grew to a point at which strong client resistance became inevitable. Although firms have grown more cautious in raising rates since the recession, clients have continued to push back strongly with demands for discounts and other forms of concessions. Accordingly, law firms have a limited ability to raise rates as a means of increasing their revenue.

## Realization

The fifth driver of law firm profitability is realization, roughly defined as the percentage of potential revenue that the firm actually bills and receives after write-offs and discounts.

Billing realization is the billable value of work (billable hours times the billed rate) divided by the standard value of the work. For example, if an associate bills two hundred hours on a client matter in a given month and his rate is $250, the standard value of that work is $50,000. If the firm billed the full $50,000 for that work, the "billing realization" rate would be 100 percent. In reality, though, standard rates are often reduced by discounts for certain clients. Under the example above, if this particular client received a 5 percent negotiated discount, the bill would be reduced by $2,500 and the billing realization rate would be $47,500

÷ $50,000, or 95 percent. The same result would ensue if instead of giving a discount, the billing partner wrote off ten hours of the associate's time, for whatever reason, before the bill was sent.

Another measure of realization is the percentage actually collected of the total amount billed. After receiving the bill in the example above, the client might dispute the amount charged for particular tasks, and the billing partner might write off another $2,500. Assuming that $47,500 was billed per the client discount, the collection realization rate would be $45,000 ÷ $47,500, or about 95 percent, assuming the client pays that amount. If the client fails to pay, the collection realization rate would be further reduced by whatever amount was not paid.

### *Importance of Understanding Economics*

As an associate, it's helpful to know the basics of law firm economics so that you can better understand how your work translates into revenue for the firm, as well as all of the factors that must be managed in order for that to happen. As a partner, it will be important to expand this understanding as you begin to control some of the drivers of profitability. Your skills in managing client expectations and keeping clients apprised of what you're doing, for example, will help avoid write-offs that reduce realization. Your skills in managing associates can help boost their productivity. And understanding the concept of leverage will help you make staffing decisions that benefit both your clients and the interests of the firm in maintaining profitability.

# CHAPTER THREE

# Take Ownership of Everything

*A Waggoner was once driving a heavy load along a very muddy way. At last he came to a part of the road where the wheels sank half-way into the mire, and the more the horses pulled, the deeper sank the wheels. So the Waggoner threw down his whip, and knelt down and prayed to Hercules the Strong. "O Hercules, help me in this my hour of distress," quoth he. But Hercules appeared to him, and said:*

*"Tut, man, don't sprawl there. Get up and put your shoulder to the wheel."*

*The gods help them that help themselves.*

*—Aesop*[1]

Perhaps the most frequently cited attribute of successful lawyers is that they "take ownership" of everything they do. No discussion of the most valued associate or the most promising prospective partner is complete without acknowledging this essential quality.

Ownership is the difference between just doing a task that you were assigned by a partner and trying to solve a client's problems as if they were your own. It is the difference between serving diligently on a firm committee and begging off because it will consume time and show no immediate economic benefit. And it's the difference between moving through your career from assignment to assignment, job to job, reacting

---

[1] Aesop, *Hercules and the Waggoner*, in AESOP'S FABLES, http://www.aesopfables.com/cgi/aesop1.cgi?sel& HerculesandtheWaggoner (last visited Nov. 14, 2012).

to circumstances that present themselves and designing your career to be exactly what you want it to be. *Ownership* means taking personal responsibility for every project that you undertake, every client whom you serve, and every commitment that you make, as well as for your ultimate success in the practice of law. The sooner you adopt an ownership mind-set, the more likely you are to succeed in the long term.

### Developing the "Owner" Mentality

Like most careers, the practice of law requires you to grow, evolve, and adapt in order to succeed in the long term. The journey begins in law school, where you receive voluminous reading assignments, attend classes, try to make sense of the cases you read, and then apply the principles to hypothetical exam questions. In your role as a student, you receive the same assignments as everyone else in your class; you have little or no choice about who your instructors are or what assignments you receive; and you receive no extra credit for doing more work than is actually assigned. All students follow essentially the same path and have the same opportunities. You are rewarded for following instructions and doing exactly what you are asked to do.

Once you start practicing law, however, it's an entirely different ball game. You don't necessarily get the same assignments as everyone else; you do have a choice regarding for whom you work, within certain parameters; and there are tremendous rewards for going beyond the four corners of an assignment and delivering more than you promised to a client. You need to transition from a more passive, student-oriented mind-set to the proactive mind-set of a small business owner who runs a mini–law practice within your firm. If you elect not to join a law firm and instead practice on your own, then you are literally the owner of your own business and must make this transition immediately.

Just as law school didn't teach you everything you need to know to become a successful young lawyer, working as an associate doesn't necessarily teach you what you need to know to become a successful partner someday. Law firms are unlike corporate environments with vertical management structures, in which each incoming employee is the responsibility of a particular supervisor who in turn reports up the chain of command to others.

Although some firms have better training and supervisory programs than others, in most firms there will not be a particular partner who is held directly responsible for your success the way a supervisor or manager would be under a corporate management structure. In most cases, you will work for several senior lawyers, who often have no idea what other assignments you are doing for others—and don't care. This is your first clue that you cannot practice effectively with an "employee" mentality, one that assumes that some senior person is responsible for teaching you all you need to know or developing you to your fullest potential. You are the only one who knows what your workload is. You are the one who must manage it, create a pipeline of incoming assignments, find the resources you need, and seek mentors to guide you in your journey.

### Taking Ownership of Internal Clientele

Rather than viewing themselves as employees who are entitled to receive quality work assignments, training, feedback, and mentorship, the most successful associates view themselves as the owners of their own minipractice within the firm in which partners are their clients. Just as senior lawyers aren't entitled to receive work from a given client, associates aren't entitled to receive particular work assignments from partners—even though certain types of assignments may be necessary for the associate's optimal development. Rather, they must earn the work they receive from their internal clients, just as partners earn the work they receive from external clients.

Building internal clientele involves understanding and managing the various partners in a firm. One successful senior associate put it this way:

> The most valuable thing I learned as a junior associate was how to deal with certain partners. Each one is different, and has their own style and preferences. Are they detailed or big-picture? Do

they check in a lot or only at the last minute? Realize that partners have usually been practicing quite a while and aren't going to change for you. Find a way to manage them and their expectations of you.

The best way to earn repeat business is to make a good first impression. A good first impression goes a long way; a poor first impression is difficult to overcome. As a new associate, you have a brief window of opportunity to impress the partners favorably. Fair or not, partners often form strong impressions of new associates (and new lateral hires) based on very little information. Some ways to start off on the right foot include paying attention to appearance, being on time, being prepared for meetings, being courteous, exhibiting confidence, and delivering an outstanding product.

## Appearance

Pay attention to your appearance. Note the attire of the associates who interviewed you. Typically, they are well respected in the firm. If you are unsure, err on the side of overdressing rather than being too casual. Make sure that your clothes are clean and pressed and that you are well groomed. Regardless of whether your appearance "should" matter as opposed to the quality of your work, the fact is that it *will* matter.

## Timeliness

Be on time. Arrive at work at a consistent time, no later than most of the partners you work for and preferably at least half an hour earlier. Being punctual for work conveys the attitude that you care. Similarly, be on time for appointments and meetings. These will be the first observations others make of you: you can either create the image of a conscientious, diligent associate or one who doesn't care and is sloppy.

## Preparation

Be prepared for every meeting. Whenever you are invited to attend a meeting, whether with a team of lawyers or a partner giving you an assignment, find out as much as you can about the purpose of the meeting before you go, and prepare. Even if the partner didn't tell you much about the matter that he's going to ask you to work on, you will impress him if you take a few minutes to find out the general nature of the matter and ask intelligent questions about it when you go to the meeting.

## Manners

Be courteous. In your interactions with others, particularly when you are new to a firm, be extremely polite. Do not interrupt others; say "please" and "thank you" when appropriate. Most associates would be surprised at the number of negative comments partners make about associates' manners.

## Confidence

Speaking confidently and making eye contact are among the most important skills to learn in your first year as a lawyer, along with how to practice. The ability to engender confidence is vital to succeeding as a lawyer, whether you are dealing with internal or external clients. When you first begin to practice, you may feel insecure and nervous as you realize how much you don't know. You must learn to speak with credibility even when you are unsure of yourself. That doesn't mean pretending to know every answer to every question: when you don't know, sometimes you'll have to say you don't know. If you don't know the answer, do your best to show the client that you heard the question, did everything you could to find the answer, and are intensely interested in learning what you don't know. This will help you earn the client's trust and confidence.

## Product

As partners "try you out" for the first time, they will make judgments very quickly about your capability. Don't put yourself in a hole by being careless. Particularly in your first few interactions with a particular partner, be conscious of making a good impression and do everything you can to deliver an outstanding product to your client.

Keep in mind, though, that your "product" is not only the written document or oral report that you give to the partner—it's the entire experience the partner will have when working with you. Your job is not just to do an assignment. Your job is to make life easier for the person you're working with, whether that's a senior associate, a partner, or an external client. "Always keep in mind what your job is. With every partner and every client you work for, keep asking yourself, 'What can I do to make life easier for the person above me on the food chain?'"[2] Many associates make the mistake of thinking that all that matters is the deliverable or work product requested by the partner. In reality, the product includes much more: the attitude you project in taking on the assignment, the enthusiasm you show for the work, your dedication to helping the client and seeking any additional information the client may need, and your dependability in ultimately delivering what the client wanted. All of these factors weigh into the partner's desire to work with you again, just as they will later influence an external client's desire to work with you on a repeat basis.

### *Taking Ownership of Your Assignments*

Becoming an entrepreneur also means shedding the student/employee mentality of doing exactly the work assigned and no more. As a professional, your job will go far beyond listening to a client's instructions. Sometimes, in fact, the client won't even know what his problem is or how to explain it—it will be up to you to figure it out by asking good questions.

Don't view it as the partner's responsibility to give you perfect instructions when he gives you a new assignment. View it as your responsibility to get all the information you need to do an excellent job. Before the assignment meeting, review all pertinent documents and complete any preparatory work suggested by the partner. And use a checklist to make sure you ask all of the right questions:

---

[2] *Id.*

- *What is the work product you want?* Does the partner want a document, an outline, a summary, or an oral report?

- *How long do you expect the project to take?* If it's a relatively long assignment, e.g., over ten hours, check in with the partner after having spent about a third of the estimated time, to make sure you're on track and the partner knows how much time the project is actually taking.

- *How can I get in touch with you if I have questions?* Learn the preferred communication style of the partners with whom you work. Beware: Some will never check their e-mail. Some prefer to speak on the phone, some in person. Some are difficult to pin down when you need to talk to them. Try finding them at the very beginning or end of the day when they are less likely to be busy in a meeting or up against a deadline. Be assertive in this process. Remember, if you fail to assert yourself in getting a hold of the partner, it will only hurt you. Fair or not, the partner will not respond well if you fail to turn in an assignment on time or if you omit important information, using the excuse "I couldn't get a hold of you." This is part of ownership: you own the responsibility for delivering an excellent product; blaming others is not an option. Thus, regardless of the method, communication is critical. One associate put it this way:

> I got a lot of experience in delegating on a large document review. It drove me crazy—I would assign work and hear nothing from the junior associate. I had to chase them down, sometimes even call the client to find out the status and whether the work had been done. Sometimes, it had been forgotten. That taught me the delegator's perspective; so when I start on a new matter for a partner, particularly one I haven't worked with before, I make sure we talk up front about the way we're

going to communicate, how frequently, and exactly what he expects me to do. Then I make sure to keep him in the loop.

- *What is the deadline for completion?* Don't leave the partner's office without knowing what time constraints he is under with regard to the client and when he is expecting your assignment to be completed. If you start to believe, for any reason, that you won't be able to meet the deadline, tell the partner as soon as possible.

With this information in hand, you should be well equipped to deliver the product that the partner wants and, ideally, to exceed his expectations.

As you're doing the work, think about additional ways to add value, both for the partner who assigned the work and for the client whom you both are serving. Consider potentially related problems and issues that may be presented by the context. The more experienced you become, the more value you'll be able to add by making observations and suggestions about issues that the partner hadn't considered. The longer you practice law, the more you'll develop the creativity and imagination that will draw clients to you and engender their loyalty.

If it's an ongoing project, ask if there is any follow-up work that you can do (for example, turning a memo analyzing potential claims into a complaint that can be filed). Always try to think of what the next step in the process will be and how the partner is going to use what you gave him. The more you can anticipate what your client will need, the more satisfied he will be with your work.

Some partners will give useful feedback on some or all projects that you do for them. Others will not. It's important to actively seek out feedback and find out what you need to do better in the future. In some cases, you'll deliver the product to the partner in the context of a meeting when you can discuss it immediately. Other times, you'll have to send it to the partner via e-mail or leave it on his desk. Regardless, make sure you find an opportunity to talk to him and make sure that he was satisfied with the work. Don't assume that no news is good news: assuming that a partner was satisfied with an assignment when he was not is dangerous, and can come back to bite you at evaluation time. Take the step of either stopping by the partner's office or setting up an appointment to talk about the project. If the partner was not satisfied, at least you'll know what he didn't like and have the ability to improve if you're given another opportunity to work with him. If you are confused about why he didn't like your work, consider talking to a fellow associate who knows the partner well. Finding out the preferences, focus, and style of each partner will allow you to serve them in the way they want to be served.

### Taking Ownership of External Clients

You also need to take ownership when dealing with external clients of the firm. This doesn't mean "stealing" them and trying to make them your own; it means doing your best to give the clients the best possible service and treating their problems with the same care and urgency you would if they were your own problems. As another associate suggested:

> Take responsibility for understanding the whole matter. Be like an investigator: find out who is working on it, what they are doing, who has what role. Constantly ask, "What are the client's business goals?" Ask questions or you won't understand enough to be really useful. If you ask a lot of questions, you'll understand more, get pulled deeper into the matter, and get better work in the long run.

Given the complexity of law practice, particularly today, it's naive to think that you'll always know the answers to questions asked by a client. Many times, you will have no idea what the answer is. Make sure, though, that you convey caring and inspire confidence. You won't do that if you shrug off responsibility for earnestly trying to help a client solve his problem.

When the client calls you with a question that you can't answer, don't immediately say that you can't help him. Take the time to ask questions and try to better understand the client's immediate problem or concern. Don't ever say, "That's not my area," or suggest that you have no duty to try and help the client. If worse comes to worst, elicit as much information as you can, repeat what the client has told you (so the client knows that you at least understand the question), summarize what you heard to confirm that you got it right, and tell the client that you'll get back to him.

There is an art to client counseling, and you won't master it the first time you speak to a client. Be prepared to practice, practice, practice. Take advantage of opportunities to volunteer for "call a lawyer" programs from time to time. This gives you practice in listening to a client, repeating the key facts, and trying to offer some helpful advice even if you don't have the precise answer to the client's question. It's important to show the client that you care about his problem. This is another form of ownership—not passing the client off on someone else but walking him through the problem as much as you can. Sometimes the client will realize that the real issue is different from his initial question. Client counseling is a highly valuable skill to have, as often the biggest differentiator for a client among attorneys who are competing for his business is the degree to which they simply care about that client.

There is no worse feeling than to be a client seeking help and have the attorney respond by saying, essentially, "Sorry—there's nothing I can do." That should *never* be your answer to a client. Even if you have to give your client bad news or the answer to a client's particular question is no, you can always find something useful to say to the client. Say something that shows you heard, you care about the client's issues, and you will find some way to help, even if it's not in the particular way that the client had in mind. That way, you show the client that you are invested in helping him (or his business) succeed and that you are in the trenches with him.

### Owning Your Career

Another form of ownership is taking charge of your career. In your early years, you don't always have many choices about the partners you work for or the assignments you are given. But as you begin to build credibility, more people—even those outside your immediate practice area—will want to work with you, and this will give you options.

Think about the type of work you ultimately would like to do and the kinds of clients for whom you would like to work. Seek out work from the partners who do what you want to do for the type of clients you want to work for. Do some independent research on which practice areas look promising for the future, and make a plan to develop your practice in that direction. Don't just float along from assignment to assignment waiting to see what kind of work you get or for whom you end up working.

The associate who owns his career makes active decisions about where he wants it to go. He researches and keeps his eyes and ears open to identify the practice area in which he eventually wants to focus. He attends educational programs and conferences—even at his own expense, if necessary—to learn more about the practice area. He calls prominent lawyers in the practice area and asks them to join him for coffee or informational interviews to discuss how they went about creating their own career paths.

### The Benefits of Ownership

The reason that "taking ownership" is such a prized characteristic in associates is that, unfortunately, many associates lack this mind-set. Associates who do not take ownership have an attitude of entitlement, expecting to be given all that they need in order to succeed without having to seek it out. These associates do what they are asked to do on their work assignments, but they go no further and don't put themselves into the client's mind-set. When things go wrong, they blame others—the prior associates on the matter, staff members, and even on occasion the partners for whom they work. They complain and treat problems as if they are everyone else's problems but not their own. Partners quickly tire of these attitudes.

The practice of law is the art of making judgment calls, sometimes hundreds of times a day. It is not an exact science, there are rarely black-and-white answers, and some things that you try are not going to work.

As a lawyer, you cannot offer your client certainty. But you will engender confidence and loyalty in your clients by standing behind your decisions, owning them, embracing the client's cause, and showing that you are "in it" with them all the way. This applies not only to external clients, who come to the firm with legal problems, but to internal clients, i.e., partners who need to rely on you to cover their backs, help them look good to their clients, and keep them from making careless mistakes.

Cultivating an attitude of ownership is a two-sided coin. On the one hand, it can be scary to put yourself out there, to take responsibility for your recommendations and actions, to actively seek out a particular career path, and to risk being wrong. On the other hand, there is nothing more fulfilling than receiving a client's undying gratitude and loyalty when you fight in the trenches with him, take a stand, follow a path, and end up being right.

---

### "Taking Ownership" Checklist

1. Think like an owner, not an employee.
2. Build your own minipractice within the firm and develop internal clients.
3. Provide the best possible experience for your clients when they give you work.
4. Take initiative to seek out the kind of work you want and to keep busy.
5. Stay conscious of the attitude that you're conveying—it matters more than you think.
6. If you make a mistake, don't make excuses and don't blame others. Accept responsibility and make it right.
7. Go beyond doing just what you're told. Put yourself in the clients' shoes and think of more ways to help them.

# CHAPTER FOUR

# Stay Humble

*Humility is knowing we're going to get kicked (and when we least
expect it) and striving to get kicked differently each time. Arrogance
is thinking that no one would ever dare take aim.*

—*Erika Napoletano*[1]

Lawyers can be arrogant and often don't realize it. Some would
argue that lawyers are predisposed to arrogance, both because those who
choose to be lawyers tend to be competitive, dispassionate, and
extremely confident and because their training further encourages them
to be skeptical, critical, and opinionated.[2] Whatever its roots, arrogance
can sabotage your career unless you become aware of how you communicate with others, seek feedback on how you come across, and actively
cultivate an air of humility.

In some respects, law firm associates live in a sheltered world. Unlike
their cohorts who strike out on their own, law firm associates typically
have a buffer (in the form of supervising partners) between themselves
and clients, courts, opposing counsel, firm decision makers, and other
sources of potentially harsh judgment and consequences. Unscathed by
the wounds of battle on the frontlines, they may develop overconfidence
or, worse, arrogance.

---

[1] Erika Napoletano, *Humility: An Undervalued but Crucial Business Asset*, ENTREPRENEUR (May 24, 2011),
http://www.entrepreneur.com/article/219613 (last visited Nov. 15, 2012).

[2] Douglas B. Richardson, *A Case Study in Arrogance: Diagnosing and Addressing Lawyers' Most Common Blind Spot*,
ALTMAN WEIL REPORT TO LEGAL MGMT. 4, 4 (June 2006).

Having been told repeatedly that they are smart, good writers or drafters, and valuable team members, some young associates start to think that they have it made. Some "superstars" see their fellow associates getting involved in community service organizations, writing articles, becoming active in bar associations, and attending networking events without receiving an immediate payoff in return, so they don't believe that these efforts are necessary. Instead, they place their entire focus on billable work to the exclusion of the other skill sets, assuming that will carry them for the indefinite future.

This is a dangerous attitude to adopt. If left unchecked, an overly inflated ego can reduce associates' motivation to develop; prevent them from assessing themselves realistically; interfere with peer and staff relationships; and, ultimately, impair their ability to practice law effectively.

Because of these dangers, senior lawyers need to avoid lavishing too much praise on associates without also counseling them about the areas in which they need to develop. Caught up in the victory of a successful deal closing or winning a case, partners can get carried away with their praise. They are doing the young lawyers a disservice, however, by not also (even in a separate conversation) telling them that it's important to focus on leadership, management, and people skills as well. Young lawyers should actively seek to strike a balance between accepting praise and encouragement and knowing that they must continually improve. As Miles Cortez, a corporate executive and former senior partner, so aptly stated in addressing a class of new lawyers: "Don't take yourself too seriously. Let me be blunt. The fact is you're twice as good as your critics think you are and half as good as your Mom thinks you are. Your mission is to strive to prove your Mom is closer to correct than your critics are."[3]

Those who stay humble, hungry to prove themselves, and appreciative of the opportunities they've received set in motion an upward spiral of ever-increasing accomplishment, successful interpersonal relationships, and satisfaction with their careers.

---

[3] Interview with Miles Cortez, Corporate Counsel, Aimco, in Denver, Colo.

## *The Price of Arrogance*

### Encouraging Complacency and Lack of Growth

Arrogance can cause you to overestimate your own opinions and judgments and to resist modifying them when evidence suggests that they aren't correct. In a 2011 article in the *New York Times Magazine,* psychologist and economics Nobel laureate Daniel Kahneman described an early encounter with this phenomenon. Assigned to observe a leadership assessment exercise, he was so sure of his predictions about the participants' leadership capabilities that he disregarded indisputable data proving him wrong, over and over again.[4] Noting that "[o]verconfidence arises because people are often blind to their own blindness," Kahneman concluded that "true intuitive expertise is learned from prolonged experience with good feedback on mistakes."[5]

With respect to law firm associates, overconfidence causes them to believe that all they have to do is continue what they've been doing, and their careers will be made. This costly error not only makes them focus too narrowly on the skills for which they've been receiving praise, it can cause them to become complacent and neglect career development altogether. The most highly acclaimed associates are often the ones most frequently absent from in-house training programs and the ones who are least likely to seek advice on how to build their careers.

### Damaging or Preventing Relationships with Colleagues

Another consequence of arrogance in the workplace is that it carries "negative socioemotional consequences . . . such as being liked and respected less, and judged more deserving of failure."[6] In 2010, a group of organizational psychologists published the results of a four-year study on arrogant behavior in the workplace. Under the Workplace Arrogance

---

[4] Daniel Kahneman, *Don't Blink! The Hazards of Confidence*, N.Y. TIMES MAG. #, 2 (Oct. 19, 2011), *available at* http://www.nytimes.com/2011/10/23/magazine/dont-blink-the-hazards-of-confidence.html?pagewanted=all (last visited Nov. 15, 2012).

[5] *Id.* at 6.

[6] Russell E. Johnson et al., *Acting Superior but Actually Inferior? Correlates and Consequences of Workplace Arrogance*, 23 HUM. PERFORMANCE 403, 422 (2010).

Scale (WARS) that they constructed, high scores were associated with high social dominance and trait anger, and also with narcissistic tendencies such as entitlement and superiority.[7] More to the point, results consistently revealed that arrogance is significantly and negatively related to task performance and citizenship behaviors.[8]

If you want successful relationships with your colleagues, check your ego at the door. Associates who convey the attitude that they are superior to their peers can find themselves without support in times of need and without access to valuable tips about how to navigate the firm, how to adapt to working with particular partners, and how to do certain types of assignments.

---

Jerry H. was a third-year associate at a large law firm. In his second year, he had two successful summary judgment motions and second-chaired a trial with an influential partner. He received great reviews, and word about his abilities spread quickly among the partners. Demand for Jerry's work went up, and he got busier, receiving even more praise from his new internal clients.

The praise went to his head. Jerry figured that he was on the fast track to partnership, that he was "in" with the important partners; he decided that at every firm event, he should focus his attention solely on partners rather than fellow associates. When invited to have beers after work with the other associates, Jerry declined, feeling that he had nothing to learn from them and would be better served by asking partners out for drinks or lunches.

One day, one of the name partners in the firm, whom Jerry had never met, went to Jerry's office. The partner asked him to do a special project, evaluating a particularly thorny zoning problem for an important client. Jerry knew better than to blow the opportunity by saying he knew nothing about zoning law (his practice focused on mergers and acquisitions), so he eagerly agreed to do the work for the name partner, who needed an answer by the close of the next business day.

---

[7] *Id.*

[8] *Id.*

Jerry began poring over the file, trying to figure out where to begin in solving the zoning problem. He realized that he would need to spend several hours reading treatises and overview articles just to get the lay of the land before actually finding the law on the client's problem. However, Jerry remembered that his fellow associate, Mark Y., had extensive experience with planning and zoning issues.

With Mark's guidance, Jerry could have done an excellent job on the project, and submitted his memo on time. But Jerry had alienated Mark with his superior attitude. After not receiving a response to an e-mail that Jerry had sent to Mark two hours earlier, Jerry called Mark. Mark didn't take the call, and he didn't return the call. By the end of the day, Jerry knew that he would not be able to get help from Mark. Jerry struggled, learned as much as he could that night and the next morning, and put together an average memo for the name partner, which he turned in at the end of the day. Unimpressed, the name partner never gave Jerry another assignment. When discussing Jerry with other partners, he told them he didn't see what all the hype was about.

Jerry's story is just one example of how arrogance can interfere with personal relationships. No one can ever master the law completely, and everyone needs help from others at times. Make no comparisons between yourself and others, value the talents and strengths that your peers possess, and stay humble about your own accomplishments if you want to succeed.

### Making Mistakes in Advising Clients

Because they are so well educated and intellectually adept, lawyers often forget that they are in a service business. They treat the client as though he is fortunate to have the benefit of their wisdom. Clients don't like this, and too much arrogance can keep a client from ever hiring you in the first place.

If the client does get past the arrogance, a lack of humility can interfere with effective client service. Just as arrogance can cause you to overestimate your opinion of your professional stature, it can cause you to answer a difficult client question too confidently, without confirming the answer through careful research. There is a balancing act that must take place when advising clients. Although clients want their lawyers to inspire confidence, overconfidence can cause a lawyer to make careless mistakes. There is no worse way to lose credibility than to be forced to contact a client to say that your first answer was wrong and that, upon further review, there was a better answer or a more sound recommendation that you could have made.

## Alienating Clients and Increasing the Risk of Malpractice Claims

As one might expect, arrogance can have the affect of alienating clients. Just as arrogant behaviors can impair relationships with coworkers, they can be off-putting to clients as well. Not only can arrogance cause you to lose clients, it can also actually increase your risk of malpractice claims.

As Malcolm Gladwell discussed in his best-selling book *Blink*, the risk of a professional being sued actually has little to do with how many mistakes the professional makes. Research on medical malpractice lawsuits shows that there are highly skilled doctors who get sued frequently, and there are doctors who make many mistakes yet never get sued.[9] The differentiating factor is how the patients were treated by their doctors. Those who were rushed, ignored, or otherwise treated poorly were more likely to sue. On the other hand, patients whose doctors took time to talk with them, listened to them, and treated them with respect were highly unlikely to sue.

This dynamic would apply to any professional relationship in which a client reposes trust in a professional. You are more likely to give someone the benefit of the doubt when you like them and more likely to become angry about a professional's mistake if you were poorly treated by that person. As articulated by the authors of *The Trusted Advisor*, "[t]here is no greater source of distrust than advisors who appear to be

---

[9] MALCOLM GLADWELL, BLINK: THE POWER OF THINKING WITHOUT THINKING 40 (Little, Brown 2005).

more interested in themselves than in trying to be of service to the client."[10]

### *Humility and Leadership*

Arrogance also impairs your ability to persuade and lead others. Research has shown that the most effective leaders blend "extreme personal humility with intense professional will."[11] A strong leader exhibits characteristics of humility by conducting himself in the following ways:

- demonstrates a compelling modesty, shunning public adulation and never being boastful

- acts with quiet, calm determination; relies principally on inspired standards, not inspiring charisma, to motivate

- channels ambition into the company, not the self; sets up successors for even more greatness in the next generation

- looks in the mirror, not out the window, to apportion responsibility for poor results, never blaming other people, external factors, or bad luck[12]

Fortunately, arrogance can be unlearned through increased self-awareness, strengthening of your core skills (as studies show that arrogance often results from low self-confidence and actual poor performance), and sensitivity to your impact on others. When those who are led attribute humility to their leaders, they also perceive the leader as more honest, trustworthy, competent, and confident.[13] So give credit generously to others, take responsibility when you make a mistake, and check your ego at the door if you want to maximize your likelihood of reaching long-term success.

---

[10] David H. Maister, Charles H. Green & Robert M. Galford, The Trusted Advisor 80 (Free Press 2000).

[11] Jim Collins, *Level 5 Leadership: The Triumph of Humility and Fierce Resolve*, Harv. Bus. Rev. 2 (Jan. 2001).

[12] *Id.* at 7.

[13] Rob Nielsen, Jennifer A. Marrone & Holly S. Slay, *A New Look at Humility: Exploring the Humility Concept and Its Role in Socialized Charismatic Leadership*, 17 J. Leadership & Organizational Stud. 33, # (2010).

### Are you Arrogant? Top Ten Arrogant Behaviors

1. Believes that he/she knows better than everyone else in any given situation.
2. Makes decisions that impact others without listening to their input.
3. Uses non-verbal behaviors like glaring or staring to make people uncomfortable.
4. Criticizes others.
5. Belittles his/her employees publicly.
6. Asserts authority in situations when he/she does not have the required information.
7. Discredits others' ideas during meetings and often makes those individuals look bad.
8. Shoots down other people's ideas in public.
9. Exhibits different behaviors with subordinates than with supervisors.
10. Makes unrealistic time demands on others.

Excerpted [obtain permission] from *Workplace Arrogance Scale*, *in* Russell E. Johnson et al., *Acting Superior but Actually Inferior?: Correlates and Consequences of Workplace Arrogance*, 23 HUM. PERFORMANCE 403, 427 (2010), *available at* www.tandfonline.com/doi/full/io.1080/08959285.2010.515279.

# CHAPTER FIVE

# Assess Yourself

*From the get-go, you need to figure out: Where is your place in the business? Recognize that law is a business and you need to decide where your strengths are, what role you want to play, and how you fit in. Figure out who the successful lawyers are, who you want to emulate.*

—*Cristal DeHerrera*[1]

There are many ways to increase your value to a firm. As you prepare for the years ahead, take a hard look at what you have to offer, how you come across to others, and what areas merit the most attention in your ongoing development efforts. Seek out feedback on your performance, accept the feedback you receive, and resist the urge to be defensive. Without gaining a realistic understanding of your strengths and weaknesses and an awareness of how you impact others, it will be difficult to realize your maximum effectiveness as a lawyer and a partner.

### Take an Inventory of Your Skill Sets

As a starting point, complete an evaluation of yourself on the five fundamental skill sets. If your firm has a self-evaluation form, start there; if not, use the checklist at the end of this chapter as a guide (Form 1). Whatever form you use, the key is to be as honest with yourself as you can be. Review your performance in each of the listed skill categories and assign a development priority to each one. Use "Other" for

---

[1] Interview with Cristal DeHerrera, Senior Assoc., Brownstein Hyatt Farber Schreck, LLP, in Denver, Colo.

any skills or abilities you've been asked to develop or have identified yourself that aren't listed on the chart.

In most cases, the development priorities will be higher for those skills that need the most work and lower for those in which you are already strong. For example, if you consistently receive feedback that writing is a strength for you, then developing this skill would be a low priority. That doesn't mean that you don't need to continuously focus on writing well and take opportunities to strengthen your writing skills; but in terms of timing, you might start with other skills first. If it has been suggested that you get more experience in public speaking, "Oral Communication" might be a high-priority development area for you. In the "Comments" column, note any particular feedback you've received in that area and a general note or two about how you might address your development in that area.

### Make a Practice Development Plan

Once you've completed the self-assessment, think about feedback that you've received from supervising lawyers, peers, and those you supervise. Make notes in the areas provided in the inventory, and highlight the priority areas in which you want to focus your development. Use the information in the inventory to create a development plan (Form 2 at the end of this chapter). Use the development plan to add action items to your active projects list (see next section), and make a recurring entry on your electronic calendar to review and revise your development plan monthly.

Then take your plan to a supervisor, mentor, or other senior lawyer whose judgment you trust. Ask that person if he can take the time to review your plan with you and whether he can suggest any areas for development or specific action steps that you may have overlooked.

As you begin to develop your plan, it will become apparent to you that you need to spend a lot more time on your career than the eighteen hundred–plus hours you're expected to bill every year. Many law firm associates complain that they are expected to participate in training sessions and attend events for which they don't get billable-hour credit. If that is your mind-set, it needs to change. In addition to the billable-hour requirement of your firm, you should plan to spend at least three hundred additional hours on your career each year, which will include time spent developing yourself as a lawyer, contributing to the firm, and building your profile in the community. In fact, a "model diet" of annual hours has been described by the ABA Commission on Billable Hours as including nineteen hundred hours per year of billable client work, one hundred hours of pro bono work, one hundred hours of service to the firm, seventy-five hours of client development, seventy-five hours of training and professional development, and fifty hours of service to the profession.[2]

Accordingly, to make your planning easier, the development plan form includes an hours budget at the top. As you start your plan, think about how much time you will be able to devote to the various components and budget your time accordingly.

### Create and Maintain an Active Projects List

Another way to assess and track your work is to create an active projects list (Form 3 at the end of this chapter), listing every matter on which you are assigned to work. Include in the list not only billable projects but also nonbillable work you are doing on firm committees, for nonprofit organizations, and for your own business and professional development. This will help you integrate the planning of all of your professional activities and enable you to see at a glance your priorities, deadlines, and overall workload. Make a recurring entry on your electronic calendar to review and update your active projects list weekly, perhaps on Friday afternoons. The list will then feed into your daily to-do list and help you prioritize individual tasks.

In addition to helping you organize your work, the active projects list has an additional benefit. Every forty-five to ninety days, depending on how frequently you add and delete matters from your list, save a copy in either a paper or electronic file. Eventually, you will create an archive of these lists, which document your experience, the matters you've

---

[2] *See* AM. BAR ASS'N, ABA COMMISSION ON BILLABLE HOURS REPORT 50 (Aug. 2002).

worked on, the kinds of tasks you've performed, and with whom you've worked. You can refer to this archive when called upon to update your firm bio or representative matters lists, when completing your self-evaluation at review time, or when creating cover letters and résumés.

### Assess Your Image

Another area in which you need to make an honest self-assessment is the impression you make on others through your actions, mannerisms, and appearance. Your image is not only conveyed by the way you look and sound, it's also conveyed by the manners you use, the consideration you show for others, and the discretion you show in handling information. Realize that your image is built over a long period of time through repeated interactions with the same people (for example, partners in your firm).

If put together with careful thought and authenticity, your image can enhance your personal brand, give you extra credibility and confidence, and reinforce the positive assumptions that people make when they interact with you. If neglected, your image can work against you and distract others from the substance of what you say and do. A poor professional image can cause people to underestimate you and create a psychological hurdle for them to overcome in placing their trust and confidence in you. Fair or not, power and credibility go to those who make good impressions.

Take the quick inventory at the end of this chapter (Form 4) to determine whether there is anything you can work on to improve your image. Some of these items bear additional discussion.

### Dressing Well

Many young associates resist the notion of improving their image. They believe it shouldn't matter how they look as long as they are smart and competent. "It's the substance that matters, not the surface," they opine. They are determined to convey their individuality, believing they are being courageous in defying the conventionality of traditional office dress codes. They create barriers for themselves, however, when this individuality attracts negative attention and undermines the professionalism and intelligence they have to offer. For example, female associates who wear short skirts, tight clothing, and low necklines might not be taken seriously by older partners. Whether it "should" matter or not, people form impressions by the way you look, and they make assumptions based on those impressions. If you want people to assume that you are smart, competent, and capable, you need to dress the part.

Keep in mind that as a lawyer, you are a leader. You are someone whom people, even powerful people, look to for advice. Clients trust lawyers with some of their deepest secrets, both business and personal. In short, you are expected to convey a higher degree of knowledge and credibility than workers in other occupations. Clients want their lawyers to be the best-dressed people in the room because this reflects confidence, capability, and attention to detail. When in doubt about how to dress, go half a step more formal.

### Focusing on Body Language and Voice Characteristics

For many people, it's difficult to believe that superficial impressions can have a substantively negative effect on a person. But they do. In his studies of body language, Dr. Albert Mehrabian found that only 7 percent of the emotional meaning in a message is perceived based on the words we use. Approximately 38 percent is communicated through the tone and inflection of our voice, and 55 percent is communicated nonverbally through facial expression, gestures, and posture.[3] Reading these nonverbal cues, people form impressions of us very quickly, and if there is a contradiction between the nonverbal message and the words you use, the nonverbal message will carry *the* greatest impact. This is true not only for salespeople selling a product and politicians speaking in a debate but also for lawyers giving the first words of an opening statement or meeting a potential client for the first time.

---

[3] ALBERT MEHRABIAN, SILENT MESSAGES: IMPLICIT COMMUNICATION OF EMOTIONS AND ATTITUDES # (Wadsworth 1981) (currently distributed by Albert Mehrabian, am@kaaj.com).

## Actively Listening

Being an active listener conveys the impression that you are interested, intelligent, and attentive. Lawyers are often tempted to show others how much they know and how quickly they can grasp the critical elements of a problem and prescribe a solution. This is one of the qualities that people hate about lawyers—they seem much more interested in themselves than in the people around them. Distinguish yourself from these stereotypical lawyers and listen carefully, whether you are talking to a colleague in your firm, another member of the bar, or a potential client. Ask thoughtful questions that show you heard the speaker. As Dale Carnegie once said, "you can make more friends in two months by becoming interested in other people than you can in two years by trying to get other people interested in you." (D. Carnegie, How to Win Friends and Influence People, 1937).

## Avoiding Gossip and Other Inappropriate Communication

When you belong to any group, there are opportunities for gossiping about other group members, particularly those who are not popular at a given moment. As a lawyer, it is particularly important for you to resist this temptation. First, it hurts your image and credibility in general. As is commonly said, "big people talk about ideas. Average people talk about things. Small people talk about other people." Second, it can backfire on you, as your comments may be repeated out of context to others or, worse, to the person who was the brunt of the gossip. That could kill any potential for establishing a friendship or even a collegial relationship with that person. Third, even if someone else starts the gossip and you merely chime in or agree, the very person who started the gossip will see you differently and possibly lose a degree of respect for you.

On a related note, lawyers can also undermine their credibility by disclosing the secrets and confidences of others as well as too much information (TMI) about themselves.

Avoid these behaviors. Once you are branded as someone with poor judgment, you may not only be excluded from sensitive information, but you may also be passed over for valuable work assignments and committee positions.

## Choosing an Optimal Mode of Communication

In our busy world, it can sometimes be tempting to use e-mail almost exclusively. It is expedient, cost-effective, and generally nonobtrusive.

However, both your internal and external clients will have preferences as to their mode of communication for various purposes, with some preferring e-mail and some preferring to talk on the telephone, depending on the circumstances. Respect these preferences.

In addition, think about the message that you are sending in a particular instance and determine which mode of communication will be most effective: an in-person visit, a telephone call, or an e-mail. When a conversation involves sensitive information or the delivery of bad news, an in-person or telephone discussion will almost always be more effective. Remember that e-mail prevents the recipient from receiving nonverbal cues, picking up nuances, and sometimes hearing the empathy that you could convey through your voice. It can also lead to misunderstandings. Particularly if a disagreement starts to arise in the course of an e-mail correspondence, consider making a telephone call to avoid escalating the dispute further and to put everyone back on their best behavior.

## Keeping Promises

Each time you keep your commitment to attend a meeting, arrive on time for an appointment or meeting, and deliver what you promised, you reinforce a positive, credible image of yourself. Conversely, each time you fail to show up for an appointment, break a commitment, or deliver less than you promised, you undermine your image. It takes multiple positive experiences to offset one negative experience, so don't put yourself in a hole.

Many young lawyers underestimate the damage that canceling plans can do to their reputation and the way in which they're perceived, particularly by older partners. For example, some commit to attending a firm event or filling a table at a charity function and then fail to show up. They may call with an excuse, often saying they "have too much work to do," but they don't realize they are hurting their image in the eyes of the people to whom they committed. If you do this too many times, you will be branded as a no-show and potentially excluded from future events that could present great opportunities. Yes, sometimes you will have to cancel, and doing this once in a great while is not likely to damage your image. But as a rule, make every effort not to commit to something unless you're fairly certain you can keep your commitment.

## Form 1
## Skill Set Inventory

| Skill Set | Low Priority | Medium Priority | High Priority | Comments |
|---|---|---|---|---|
| **Legal Skills** | | | | |
| Written Communication | | | | |
| Oral Communication | | | | |
| Legal Analysis | | | | |
| Substantive Legal Knowledge | | | | |
| Other (describe) | | | | |
| **Business Development** | | | | |
| Internal (in-firm) Networking (e.g., attending events; extending invitations to lunch, coffee, etc.; actively building relationships) | | | | |
| External Networking (e.g., attending events; extending invitations to lunch, coffee, etc.; actively building relationships) | | | | |
| Identifying One or More Practice Niches | | | | |
| Writing Articles on Area(s) of Expertise | | | | |
| Speaking in Area(s) of Expertise | | | | |
| Other (describe) | | | | |

| Skill Set | Low Priority | Medium Priority | High Priority | Comments |
|---|---|---|---|---|
| **Client Relations** | | | | |
| Keeping Clients Advised of Matter Status | | | | |
| Including Clients in Key Decisions | | | | |
| Sending Clients Information They May Find Useful | | | | |
| Checking in with Clients Periodically About Satisfaction | | | | |
| Looking for Opportunities to Visit Clients' Offices or Worksites | | | | |
| Building Relationships with Client Contacts at My Level | | | | |
| Looking for New Ways to Help Existing Clients | | | | |
| Checking in with Clients Not Currently Being Represented | | | | |
| Other (describe) | | | | |
| **Practice Management** | | | | |
| Capturing All Billable Time, Recording It Promptly, and Communicating the Value of My Work in My Entries | | | | |
| Scheduling and Time Management | | | | |
| Delegating Appropriately to Junior Lawyers and Staff | | | | |
| Juggling Multiple Matters and Clients Effectively; Staying Organized | | | | |
| Other (describe) | | | | |

| Skill Set | Low Priority | Medium Priority | High Priority | Comments |
|---|---|---|---|---|
| **Leadership** | | | | |
| Serving in a Leadership Role Within the Firm | | | | |
| Serving in a Leadership Role for a Community or Nonprofit Organization | | | | |
| Providing Timely and Accurate Feedback to Those to Whom I Delegate | | | | |
| Thinking of Ways to Expand the Development of Those to Whom I Delegate | | | | |
| Other (describe) | | | | |

## Form 2
### Practice Development Plan

Name: _____

Effective Period: _____

Practice Area: _____

**Time-Allocation Plan**

<u>Billable</u>-hours goal for fiscal year:                                    _____

To meet this goal, I need to average ___ billable hours per week and ___ per month.

<u>Nonbillable</u>-hours goal for fiscal year:                           _____

Target allocation of nonbillable hours:

**Pro Bono Work**                                                          _____

**Professional Development**                                          _____
(attending training, seeking coaching, professional reading, etc.)

**Business Development**                                                _____
(networking, growing relationships, building reputation and visibility,
creating a practice niche, etc.)

**Community Involvement**                                            _____
(volunteering for projects, serving on nonprofit boards,
attending fund-raisers, etc.)

**Service to the Firm**                                                  _____
(recruiting, mentoring junior associates, serving on firm committees, etc.)

**Service to the Profession**                                          _____
(serving professional organizations and bar associations;
mentoring outside the firm; representing lawyers at career fairs; etc.)

<u>TOTAL</u> number of hours I will invest in my career this year
(billable + nonbillable):                                                  _____

## Professional Development Activities

### I.    Legal Skills
(e.g., written communication, oral communication, research and analysis, advocacy, negotiation, substantive knowledge)

| Skill or Knowledge to Be Developed | Action Steps to Be Taken | Timeline |
|---|---|---|
|  |  |  |
|  |  |  |
|  |  |  |

### II.    Practice Management
(e.g., time management, organizational skills, law firm economics, case or deal management)

| Skill or Knowledge to Be Developed | Action Steps to Be Taken | Timeline |
|---|---|---|
|  |  |  |
|  |  |  |
|  |  |  |

### III.    Leadership
(e.g., delegation, supervision, mentoring, leading a team)

| Skill or Knowledge to Be Developed | Action Steps to Be Taken | Timeline |
|---|---|---|
|  |  |  |
|  |  |  |
|  |  |  |

## Business Development Activities

### I.    Building My Profile
(giving presentations, writing articles, teaching educational programs, participating in industry groups, etc.)

| Goal | Action Steps to Be Taken | Timeline |
|------|--------------------------|----------|
| Goal 1: | | |
| Goal 2: | | |
| Goal 3: | | |

### II.   Networking
(attending events, meeting new people, connecting people who can help each other, building your Rolodex, etc.)

| Goal | Action Steps to Be Taken | Timeline |
|------|--------------------------|----------|
| Goal 1: | | |
| Goal 2: | | |
| Goal 3: | | |

### III.  Growing Relationships
(expanding relationships with existing clients; sending helpful articles; inviting people to lunch, coffee, or events; finding new ways to help a contact; getting to know colleagues, etc.)

| Goal | Action Steps to Be Taken | Timeline |
|------|--------------------------|----------|
| Name of Contact 1: | | |
| Name of Contact 2: | | |
| Name of Contact 3: | | |

## Pro Bono and Community Involvement

I.    Pro Bono Service

| Goal | Action Steps to Be Taken | Timeline |
|------|--------------------------|----------|
|      |                          |          |
|      |                          |          |
|      |                          |          |

II.   Community Involvement

| Goal | Action Steps to Be Taken | Timeline |
|------|--------------------------|----------|
|      |                          |          |
|      |                          |          |
|      |                          |          |

## Other Goals

| Goal | Action Steps to Be Taken | Timeline |
|------|--------------------------|----------|
|      |                          |          |
|      |                          |          |
|      |                          |          |

**Form 3**

**Active Projects List**
**(as of [date])**

| Client Name | Matter | Supervising Attorney | Contacts | Status |
|---|---|---|---|---|
| Acme Widget Co. | Winthrop wage dispute<br><br>61220.023 | C. Martin<br>x1234 | Fred Jones,<br>client contact:<br>212-213-1256 | 1. Acme was served with complaint on 11/10/09.<br>2. Need to draft answer; due on **11/30/13**.<br>3. Need to research whether Winthrop was employee or independent contractor. |
| | Trump executive contract<br><br>61220.024 | C. Martin<br>x1234 | Fred Jones,<br>client contact:<br>212-213-1256 | 1. Client wants us to review executive contract proposed by new president of Acme, Jim Bayer.<br>2. We promised a recommendation by **12/2/12**.<br>3. Need to obtain copy of contract with prior CEO. |
| Big Business Machines, Inc. | Computer delivery litigation<br><br>82932.01 | R. Franco<br>x4567 | Sam Smith,<br>client contact:<br>212-509-8888 | 1. Reviewed correspondence to determine whether IBM has claim against supplier.<br>2. Conference call with client set for **12/5/12**.<br>3. Began drafting complaint; have ready in time for conference call. |
| McPatrick's Inc. | Burger Co. trademark litigation<br><br>44302.03 | B. Dunlap<br>x7890 | Joe Schmoe,<br>client contact:<br>212-598-4444<br><br>Brad Pitts,<br>counsel for codefendant Fred's Junior:<br>212-424-2444 | 1. Received Burger Co.'s discovery requests 11/24/12; responses due **12/24/12**.<br>2. Contacted client, sent copy of requests, set conference call for **12/8/12**.<br>3. Need to prepare draft discovery responses before conference call. |
| Non-Billable | | | | |
| State Bar Association | Young Lawyers Executive Council | Chair:<br>J. Frederick<br>212-329-3995 | Vice-Chair:<br>F. Poole<br>212-111-4491 | 1. Next meeting is 2/5/13.<br>2. Need to prepare suggestions for new committee projects, to present at meeting. |

## Form 4
## Image Checklist

I. **Overall Appearance**

- Don't chew gum.
- Be the best-dressed person in the room.
- Maintain good posture.
- Have a firm handshake.

II. **Mannerisms and Gestures**

- Don't hide your hands in your pockets.
- Don't sway back and forth.
- Do make eye contact.

III. **Verbal Characteristics**

- Avoid finishing a statement with an upward inflection (Valley girl–speak).
- Avoid fillers (*ah*, *um*, *er*, etc.).
- Speak clearly and enunciate; avoid garbling.

IV. **Interactions with Others**

- Be on time.
- Keep your promises.
- Avoid gossip and other inappropriate communication.
- Choose an optimal mode of communication for the situation.
- Listen, listen, listen.
- Give your full attention to the person to whom you're talking.
- Don't interrupt.

# CHAPTER SIX

# Continually Improve Your Product

*A Jay venturing into a yard where Peacocks used to walk, found there a number of feathers which had fallen from the Peacocks when they were moulting. He tied them all to his tail and strutted down towards the Peacocks. When he came near them they soon discovered the cheat, and striding up to him pecked at him and plucked away his borrowed plumes. So the Jay could do no better than go back to the other Jays, who had watched his behaviour from a distance; but they were equally annoyed with him, and told him:*

*"It is not only fine feathers that make fine birds."*

*—Aesop[1]*

Looking like a lawyer and sounding like a lawyer will only get you so far—you've got to have the substance at your core to succeed in the long run. Although the focus of this book is on all the things you need to think about other than your legal skills in order to have a successful career, make no mistake: your capability as a lawyer is the bedrock on which your entire career rests. If you don't work to become and to remain the best lawyer you can possibly be, you won't have a practice to manage or clients to serve.

Being a lawyer is not something you learn once, through a three-year degree program; it demands continual learning and practice throughout your entire career. Your substantive legal knowledge must be

---

[1] Aesop, *The Jay and the Peacock, in* AESOP'S FABLES, http://www.aesopfables.com/cgi/aesop1.cgi?sel&TheJayandthePeacock (last visited Nov. 16, 2012).

continually augmented, updated, and refined; and the skills you use to utilize that knowledge for the benefit of your clients—writing, speaking, and analysis—must be continually practiced and maintained. Ways to continually improve your legal skills include paying attention to feedback, making the most of your continuing legal education opportunities, sharing information with other lawyers in your practice area, taking advantage of pro bono opportunities, making a habit of professional reading, periodically giving presentations and writing articles, keeping a reference file, and building knowledge for the future.

Most lawyers love to learn. By consciously planning your continuing development, you'll keep your career more interesting, avoid the boredom that comes with stagnation, and enhance the product that you offer to clients.

### Feedback

As discussed in the previous chapter, the growth of your legal skills, as is true of all the other skill sets, should start with an informed perspective on where you need to improve. To focus as you make your plan to improve your product—and by *product* in this context, I mean the entire package of legal skills—don't forget to consider performance feedback that you've received. This feedback may include areas you need to work on, skills you should improve, or knowledge you should gain. It may also include encouragement to build on existing skills or to explore new areas. Regardless, your growth will benefit from some objective advice.

### Continuing Legal Education

Some lawyers view minimum continuing legal education (MCLE) requirements as a cumbersome annoyance and MCLE programs as virtually worthless. If this is your attitude, you need to look for new programs and resources. Most firms pay for their lawyers to attend educational programs, so if you're not seeking out the best training in your practice area, you're shortchanging yourself. Talk to other lawyers in your practice area to find out which programs are most valuable, have the highest-quality content, and are the most relevant to your particular practice. As part of your professional development plan, write a CLE plan that identifies a seminar or conference you will attend during each quarter of the year.

In some cases, your firm may not pay for a particular program because it's too expensive or not considered relevant by your practice group leaders. Listen to their advice; but if you have a specific reason for attending a high-quality program that fits with your long-term development plans, pay for it yourself. Don't make the mistake of ignoring it just because the firm won't pay. Your investment in yourself will be worth it.

### Networking

One of the best ways to stay on top of your game is to make a habit of regularly networking with other lawyers in your practice area. If your practice group in the firm has regular meetings, attend them. Go prepared to ask questions and contribute to the discussion in a substantive way. Outside the firm, look for opportunities to attend topical lunches, happy hours, and seminars presented by bar associations and law schools. Talk to other lawyers about new developments in the practice area and general issues you frequently encounter. Ask them how they handle problems similar to those you've faced (while speaking generally, of course, and preserving the confidentiality of your clients' information). Other lawyers can be gold mines of information.

### Pro Bono Opportunities

Pro bono work is not only your duty as a lawyer, it's good for you. It can give you experience that you won't acquire in your ordinary practice and allow you to take more responsibility for your clients than you could in paying matters.

Don't limit yourself to doing the same kind of work that you do in your practice. Consider learning a new area of law specifically for your pro bono work. For example, there is often a great need for pro bono assistance with immigration matters. Once you learn the substance, all of the skills you use in the representation will translate: You'll counsel and advise your client, practice your listening skills, and learn to give helpful advice. You may draft documents or letters to submit to a tribunal or government office. You may have to appear before a tribunal to advocate your client's position. All of these facets of pro bono work will make you a better lawyer.

### Professional Reading

In the course of a day, lawyers are bombarded with information. The trick is to identify the sources of information that will serve you best and keep you aware of current events and developments while filtering out the rest. Choose at least four to five publications to read regularly that will help you stay on top of what's going on in the profession nationally, locally, and in your practice area. If you're not sure, ask an experienced practitioner for advice. If your firm has a library department, ask the reference librarian for his suggestions.

Some lawyers find it helpful to set aside fifteen to twenty minutes at the beginning of each day for this purpose. Others prefer to save their reading for once a week. Whatever schedule you choose, avoid the temptation of interrupting what you're doing each time you receive material in print or electronically. Combine reading of multiple sources into one block of time, and you will be much more efficient in both maintaining the flow of your workday and digesting the information that you are reading.

### Presentations and Articles

Another good way to stay sharp is to give presentations on a regular basis, whether inside your firm or to bar groups, industry groups, or nonprofit organizations. Not only is this important for establishing your reputation and staying visible for marketing purposes, it also forces you to study your practice area periodically. The same is true for writing articles. Often, a well-prepared presentation can form the outline for an article or vice versa, so be sure to maximize the mileage you get from studying, gathering, and organizing the information.

### Reference Files

As you read your periodicals and absorb new information, create a system for saving that information so that you can refer back to it later. Whether in paper or electronic format, create files that allow you to store helpful information so it's at your fingertips when the issue you read about arises in your practice.

Also, keep files of significant work product, whether for the substantive information it contains or the format of the document (e.g., pleading, motion, partnership agreement, etc.) Even if your firm maintains a precedent file, keep some of your own reference documents as well, particularly your best examples.

### Future Directions

In addition to building knowledge in your current practice area, think about where you want your practice to go as you develop into a partner. Watch for trends: the development of new practice areas and niches, new industries that need special expertise, and areas in which the volume of legal work is growing. Include in your professional reading some resources on these areas so that you can increase your knowledge over time and spot opportunities to build these types of practice, whether inside your firm or to external clients, as they arise.

# CHAPTER SEVEN

# Remember That Relationships Are Everything

*Once when a Lion was asleep a little Mouse began running up and down upon him; this soon wakened the Lion, who placed his huge paw upon him, and opened his big jaws to swallow him. "Pardon, O King," cried the little Mouse; "forgive me this time, I shall never forget it: who knows but what I may be able to do you a turn some of these days?" The Lion was so tickled at the idea of the Mouse being able to help him, that he lifted up his paw and let him go. Some time after the Lion was caught in a trap, and the hunters[,] who desired to carry him alive to the King, tied him to a tree while they went in search of wagon to carry him on. Just then the little Mouse happened to pass by, and seeing the sad plight in which the Lion was, went up to him and soon gnawed away the ropes that bound the King of the Beasts. "Was I not right"? said the little Mouse.*

*"Little friends may prove great friends."*

—*Aesop*[1]

For long-term success in private practice, the most important skill that you can develop is the ability to build relationships. This skill becomes increasingly important as your career progresses.

In law school, you could theoretically have no friends or outside relationships and just go to class, study diligently, get good grades, and advance to the next level (getting a job as a lawyer). Granted, you'd

---

[1] Aesop, *The Lion and the Mouse*, in AESOP'S FABLES, http://www.aesopfables.com/cgi/aesop1.cgi?sel&TheLion andtheMouse2 (last visited Nov. 17, 2012).

increase your chances of success in law school by networking and studying with other students, but it wouldn't be absolutely necessary.

Some young associates manage to get by without the ability or inclination to form relationships beyond the communications necessary to get the work done. If you do good work and are extremely intelligent, partners may allow your legal acumen to offset your lack of social skills, at least until they start considering you for partnership.

In the midlevel to senior associate years, however, it gets harder to go it alone. Those who haven't started building relationships start to fall behind those who have. As the complexity and volume of the work increases, it becomes harder to do on your own. Even if the partner who assigns the work is good at giving instructions, there will be times when you'll do a better job if you're able to get additional guidance and advice.

It's harder to produce higher volumes of work without a good secretary working on your team. You'll have frustrations in the course of learning the practice of law that you'll want to share with peers over beer or coffee. If you haven't built relationships outside the small circle of partners for whom you do work (or worse, the single partner from whom you get all of your assignments), you won't get the variety of experience and exposure to different types of law practice challenges that you would have otherwise. To put it bluntly, associates who work actively at building and maintaining relationships have a clear advantage over those who don't.

The associates who somehow manage to rise to a senior level without strong relationship skills are further disadvantaged when partnership consideration time rolls around and only a small handful of partners knows the associates and their work. If you are one of those associates and somehow managed to make partner anyway based on the sheer brilliance of your legal work, you are in for a rude awakening down the road. Once you become a partner, almost everything you need in order to be successful must come from someone else: help from staff members and associates; internal referrals from colleagues; tips on navigating the firm's politics; potential leadership positions within your firm; and, most importantly, clients. Without the ability to build relationships, sometime in your early partnership years, it's going to dawn on you that you have no clients of your own, are highly dependent on other partners for work, have little influence over firm decisions, have trouble getting associate help, and aren't in the loop about what's going on in the legal community. That's not where you want to be.

Sole practitioners, too, become acutely aware of the need to build relationships and professional networks because even competence in their practice demands the ability to reach out to others for help and advice. No one can know everything, even within a limited practice area.

Being a lone wolf, even an extremely smart one, is not a formula for long-term success, particularly in today's legal economy. The ability to build and maintain relationships is essential to gaining knowledge, growing your career, and building a book of business. Start early to develop these relationships, maintain them authentically, and you'll have a strong foundation to build on as increased responsibilities are placed on you.

### Build Relationships Within the Firm

### Treat Staff Well

Some of your most valuable potential allies in a firm are staff members: legal assistants, paralegals, clerks, librarians, office services, and IT staff. Some associates, particularly newer ones, come out of law school and see themselves as "the boss" for the first time. Able to do beginner-level assignments without much help, they don't realize how much help they will eventually need from staff members and how much help they could immediately receive if they stayed humble and asked for it. When they do ask for help, they do so in a condescending tone, intending to make clear where they stand in the professional pecking order. They underestimate the value of staff members or, worse, treat them with disrespect.

Kendall was a bright, promising fifth-year associate. He had worked for a large company before going to law school and had a great deal of real-world knowledge and maturity for a young associate. He was smart, a fast learner, and eager to bring in clients, which he had significant potential to do in light of the contacts he'd made in his prior business experience.

There was just one problem. He was rude and condescending to assistants, paralegals, and administrative staff in the firm. Feeling that he was above them, he ordered them to perform tasks and gather information for him with a smug sense of self-satisfaction and rarely thanked them for their efforts. He was not secure enough with himself to treat them as equals.

One day, Kendall received a call from a former colleague who had a potential piece of business for him. The colleague, who worked for a property management company, needed a lawyer to do an eviction proceeding immediately, that day. Wanting to get "in the door" with this client, Kendall wanted to take on the matter even though he was too busy to do the work that particular week. Knowing that many aspects of eviction work are fairly routine and use standard forms, Kendall sent an e-mail to the paralegals in his department, asking if anyone had time to help prepare the documents for an eviction proceeding.

Wanda, a paralegal who had extensive experience in real estate litigation, had handled several evictions and was familiar with the procedure. But remembering her prior dealings with Kendall in which he gave her unnecessarily tight deadlines, little explanation or background, unclear instructions, and no gratitude for work well done, and already very busy working for other lawyers, Wanda said nothing.

After receiving no response to his e-mail in the two-hour window he had allotted nor any response to his face-to-face inquiries, Kendall had to turn the work down because he didn't have the help he needed to do the project on short notice. The client went to another lawyer, who was able to pull a team together, deliver the eviction documents that day, and earn more business from the client. The client never called Kendall again.

Don't make the mistake of underestimating the value, intelligence, and capabilities of staff members. Build relationships with staff from the first day you arrive at the firm. Discard any notion of a hierarchy in which lawyers are superior to staff, and view everyone as a team member with valuable skills and knowledge to contribute. Say hello to them in the halls. Ask them about their families. Treat them as equals.

This is particularly important with respect to your legal or administrative assistant. Most individuals in these positions are extremely bright, resourceful, and knowledgeable people who could have chosen any number of professional careers. Many of them could have been lawyers had they chosen to do so. In fact, many legal secretaries go on to law school after several years of law firm experience and, capitalizing on that experience, become exceptional lawyers. Your assistant can bail you out of a tight spot, tell you how the firm politics work, provide guidance on how to work effectively with a particular partner, and help you in hundreds of other ways. Take the time to talk to him from time to time, not viewing him solely as a worker for you but as another person. Ask about his hobbies and interests. And by all means, remember him on his birthday and over the holidays. Use those occasions as an opportunity to express your gratitude for the important work that he does.

## Bond with Fellow Associates

The practice of law is a difficult way to make a living, but having friends where you work makes it infinitely more enjoyable. It helps you put your difficulties in perspective and shows you that you're not alone in the challenges that you face.

Your fellow associates can be invaluable in providing you with guidance and support. Whether you have an assigned mentor or not, cultivate relationships with associates in your own practice group as well as in other groups. When you have what you consider to be a potentially stupid question, go to the peers with whom you are friendly. Do favors for them whenever possible, providing the same type of support you would like to receive from them.

Don't overlook the importance of attending informal happy hours with groups of associates; go whenever you are invited if you possibly can. These are opportunities for building friendships and learning about the social fabric of the firm, things you will never learn if you relate to your peers only in the office. Invite other associates to have coffee or lunch with you from time to time, and learn how their practice is similar to and different from yours. Learn who their spouses are, whether they have children, and what their most important hobbies are.

A word to the wise, however: Although it's natural to want to commiserate with your fellow associates about less-than-ideal people, decisions, or dynamics going on within the firm, avoid the temptation to gossip. It's important to listen to other associates' feelings and opinions about the firm, but if they become overly negative, be careful. From time to time, there will be associates who are failing and who will blame their lack of success entirely on the firm and/or the partners for whom they work. These associates have an interest in encouraging others to feel the same way, i.e., to validate their negative feelings. They don't like to see happy associates with good attitudes because it reminds them that they are different and suggests that their failures may be their own fault. Try to stay neutral when you encounter these associates. Be a good listener and empathize, but avoid being pulled into the firm-bashing. Joining in the bitch session can not only bring down your mood and your energy level at work, it can also affect your reputation. If there is a particular issue that you can raise and actually do something about, then consider talking about it with a partner whom you trust. But if it's just a complaint about the firm and you echo that enough times, word will get around. The more negative things you say about the firm, the more difficult it becomes for the firm's leaders to envision you as their partner someday.

### Seek Out Mentors Within the Firm

A strange aspect of law firms as organizations is their horizontal, rather than vertical, management structure. Unlike typical corporations (in which an employee reports to a supervisor, who reports to a manager, who reports to a director, etc., up a chain of command), a law firm often resembles a collection of minifirms that share resources with each other, including associates. In many cases, an associate does not "report" to any one partner but works for several at a time. No one partner is responsible for a particular associate's success; and given the demands on their time to bill hours and generate business, they are not highly incentivized to go beyond the work-delegation process and reach out to mentor associates—particularly those who do not directly benefit their practice.

You, as an associate, are the one who benefits most from a mentoring relationship. That is why you must take the initiative to build these relationships. As one senior associate put it, "Reach out for mentors a couple of years above you in experience. "They're usually more accessible than more senior partners and more tuned in to what you need to know. As a junior associate, I learned a great deal from my senior associate mentor."

When considering mentors, think about respected lawyers who practice in an area you'd like to develop someday or who have hobbies or interests outside of work similar to yours. In order to select a mentor, you need to keep your ear to the ground, talk to other associates, and watch what's going on in the firm. Who is bringing in new business? Which practice groups are expanding? Which partners might you have something in common with? You can learn these basic facts by paying attention to information that's circulated and by attending firm events. Do not miss a firm event if you can possibly avoid it. Annual picnics, holiday parties, and summer associate events provide great opportunities to mingle with partners for whom you don't ordinarily work.

Keep in mind that having more than one mentor is a good thing. One may be in your practice area and an expert in the field. One may be a great rainmaker. One may be on the law firm's management team. Each relationship has something to offer, and it is to your benefit to build these relationships.

Once you've identified a potential mentor and have determined what you have in common, ask that person to coffee. Remember that senior lawyers, particularly ones you don't work for, typically have little incentive to take an interest in your career other than their belief that it's their duty to mentor. Start by focusing on your commonalities: ask questions, but also offer information in return. For example, if you are particularly good with technology, you may offer a tip based on a problem the senior lawyer raises in the conversation. If you are an experienced mountaineer and know that the partner has recently taken up this hobby, ask the partner to talk about it and offer some tips when asked. Although initially, you stand to benefit the most from the relationship, help the partner to see your value and the potential ways in which he may benefit from knowing you someday.

Start slowly. Don't ask for too much right away. Don't bombard your chosen mentor with lunch and coffee invitations. Be judicious, keep the discussions relatively short, and don't impose too much. Over time, you will be in a better position to get advice from your mentor. Of all situations, this is one you should not approach with a sense of entitlement but, rather, with a sense of gratitude. Remember that at first, your mentor is giving a lot more value to you than you are giving to your mentor. The more the relationship develops, though, the less of an imposition it will be and the more your mentor will reach out to you.

If you take the time to cultivate this relationship over months and years, you may well turn the mentor into a sponsor who will champion your cause throughout the firm. Just remember to start small and build the relationship gradually. In the same way that a person volunteers for an organization, gets to know it, increases his role, believes in the organization more strongly, gets more deeply involved, and eventually chairs the board and serves as a tireless advocate for the cause, your mentor's belief in you and support for your career must grow over time. Sponsorship must be earned—it cannot be demanded.

## Meet Firm Leaders

Don't be afraid to build relationships with leaders of the firm, both on the administrative side and among the practicing lawyers. Look for opportunities to speak with them about their interests, get to know them, and find out what's going on at the firm from their perspective. Although many associates shy away from them, these leaders can be invaluable sources of help and information.

## Don't Put All Your Eggs in One Basket

A final word of advice on building relationships within your firm: Even if you have a relationship with a very powerful partner or two, don't rely on just one or two relationships to carry your career. You must build relationships with partners outside of your practice group and within the leadership ranks. Depending on just one or two partners is risky: if their practice declines or they fall out of favor, so do you. If they leave the firm, you have no one to speak up for you.

In addition, branching out will benefit your development. As one senior associate noted, "[b]uild[ing] relationships within the firm, particularly with people outside of your practice group, . . . will get you feedback from more different sources and on different kinds of skills, and expose you to a wider range of practice experiences."

Build relationships with a wide variety of partners through work assignments, informal social events, firm-sponsored events, and your own initiative so that they can reinforce the positive messages that your primary supervisors communicate about you throughout the firm. And, as another senior associate suggested, when you do get the opportunity to serve a new internal client, make the most of it:

> Because my practice is somewhat specialized, I get a lot of work from partners in other practice groups. When I get a new "internal client," I sit down with them and offer them a menu of options for working together and communicating on the matter—anything from my simply advising them on a limited issue to working directly with the client on the entire matter. We talk about how often they want to be updated and how involved they want to be in decisions. Then I make their project a priority, try to do a quick turnaround, and always keep them in the loop.

### Build Relationships Outside the Firm

With all of the stresses of day-to-day practice, it can be easy to lose track of the outside world and focus only on the people within your firm. But it's essential to your long-term success to build relationships outside of your firm as well. These relationships can provide you with a welcome break from your day-to-day routine, a fresh perspective on law practice, and, ultimately, potential clients and job opportunities.

## Stay in Touch with Professional Peers

Your most obvious professional peers are the first people you met as you entered the profession: your law school classmates. Keep in touch with them. Attend reunions and alumni events. Choose a handful with whom to stay in touch and to compare notes as your respective careers progress.

As you work on cases and deals with other lawyers of comparable vintage, look for those you admire. Develop a cordial working relationship with them; and when you have the opportunity, invite them to lunch or coffee. Even opposing counsel can become great friends if you separate the professional position from the personal. "When you do a deal, there's almost always someone in a supporting role like yours," observed a large law firm associate. "Invite that person to lunch or coffee. That's much easier than trying to connect with the general counsel, and much more comfortable. That's an easy way to start building connections."

Look for opportunities to get involved in the "young lawyers" section of your local or state bar association. Whether you choose only to attend functions hosted by these groups or to become actively involved in their projects and initiatives, these groups are full of young lawyers who have much in common with you and much to offer by way of support, advice, and information.

Attend happy hours and other events with friends, where you can meet your friends' friends. Peers outside of your firm can provide a reality check about your expectations of your own firm and objective advice about problems that you may encounter. They can also give you ideas for other practice areas, insights on dealing with other lawyers and judges in the community, and perspectives on other practice environments such as government and in-house positions.

In short, the more relationships you build with other lawyers of your relative experience level, the greater your access to career support, advice, information, and opportunities.

## Seek Out Mentors Outside the Firm

Although it's necessary to have at least one mentor within your firm to help you navigate the organization as well as the profession, it's also helpful to have one or more mentors outside of the firm. As you meet people in the legal or business community, identify those who have attributes you admire, who have taken a path you'd like to follow some- day, or who have achieved success in a way you'd like to emulate. Ask them if they'd be willing to meet for coffee or lunch; and when they do, ask them how they became successful. Most people are flattered by such invitations, and will provide valuable advice if you ask for it. As a female associate at a Colorado firm said, "Don't be afraid to ask for help. People will give you help when you're young—they may not be so willing when you're a partner and they think you've 'made it' already. Don't be afraid of 'no'—reach out to people you want as mentors."

## Volunteer in the Community

One of the best ways to enlarge your circle beyond the legal com- munity is to volunteer for a nonprofit organization. In addition to the positive feelings you'll get from giving back to your community, volun- teering for nonprofits can help you learn valuable skills, meet commu- nity leaders, and make new friends. Find an organization whose purpose you are passionate about. Involvement in nonprofits can provide you with an outlet for using talents and energy you don't get to use as a lawyer.

The most important thing to keep in mind, however, is to keep your commitment. Given the busy lives that lawyers lead, it's often tempting to shortchange the nonprofit. Too many lawyers join nonprofit organi- zations only to put it on their résumés. When they get busy, they skip meetings and events without giving them a second thought. This is a bad habit to develop. Be aware that this hurts your reputation and your future in the organization. At whatever level you decide to become involved in an organization, you must keep your commitments by attending meetings, attending events, adding value, and delivering on your promises.

The best way to stay motivated for your nonprofit involvement? Stay true to your values and interests. "Do what you love," the female associate said. "Be authentic in your networking by choosing organizations and groups you are passionate about. Join an organization or cause that fits you, not just one that seems advantageous."[2]

A word of caution: Don't overcommit. Once you become involved in an organization as a volunteer, the organization will want more from you, particularly if you are talented and show a high level of enthusiasm for the cause. Similarly, it may be tempting to stay on the board too long. Don't make this mistake, either. Do what you commit to do; but at the end of your term, evaluate carefully whether you can continue at the same level. Sometimes you need to move on, take a break from volunteering, and then resume again later.

## Look for Ways to Help Others

Remember that relationships are a two-way street. You should be willing to give to others all of the benefits that you hope to gain from relationships. When you hear of a job opportunity that may interest your peers, pass it on. When you read a helpful article, send it around. When you meet someone with an interest similar to that of another of your contacts, introduce them to each other. And just as you wanted the benefit of mentoring from senior lawyers, volunteer yourself to serve as a mentor to a junior lawyer or law student. Successful relationship builders make a conscious habit of helping others. The female associate continued:

> Look for ways to help all of your contacts. I sit down every week or so with a list of my contacts and go through each one thinking 'What can I do for this person?' In order to do that, you have to take the time to get to know them. Know what their goals are, what they want, and what they like. Loyalty is huge. People

---

[2] *Id.*

never forget who is nice to them and who is not, and who stops being nice to them when they've left a position of power or lost a job. Be nice to everyone. Today's intern could be tomorrow's chief of staff.

Remember that relationships are a long-term proposition. Don't expect immediate rewards or favors, and don't ignore people who aren't able to help you right now, i.e., people who have limited power. To the contrary, by focusing on whom you can help rather than who can help you, you will form some of the most satisfying relationships of your career.

## Maintain Relationships

Don't build more relationships than you can maintain. And remember that not every relationship will last forever. Over time, you'll fall out of touch with some of the people you meet both inside and outside of your firm. That's a normal process: as new people come into your network, people you don't have as much in common with anymore leave it.

As to the ten to twelve people you are actively choosing to keep in your network, however, set calendar entries to remind you to connect periodically. Read local legal periodicals with news about what other lawyers are doing. When you read about your friends and contacts, send them an e-mail and invite them to tell you more about what they're doing. As a male senior associate said, "There's no substitute for face to face contact when you want to build a relationship. When you have down time, call someone you haven't spoken to for a while and set up a lunch." The more you expose yourself to news sources and share with other people, the more information and ideas you'll receive that will be valuable for your personal use and to pass on to others.

A relationship isn't authentic if one person only contacts the other when that person needs something from the other. Don't expect help from someone you were too busy to keep in touch with for many years. Actively nurture the relationships within your network by looking for ways to help your contacts and reasons to stay in touch with them.

# CHAPTER EIGHT

# Distinguish Yourself:
# What Makes You So Special?

*A great conflict was about to come off between the Birds and the Beasts. When the two armies were collected together the Bat hesitated which to join. The Birds that passed his perch said: "Come with us"; but he said: "I am a Beast." Later on, some Beasts who were passing underneath him looked up and said: "Come with us"; but he said: "I am a Bird." Luckily at the last moment peace was made, and no battle took place, so that the Bat came to the Birds and wished to join in the rejoicings, but they all turned against him and he had to fly away. He then went to the Beasts, but soon had to beat a retreat, or else they would have torn him to pieces. "Ah," said the Bat, "I see now,*

*"He that is neither one thing nor the other has no friends."*

*—Aesop*[1]

When you emerge as a partner, you'll be expected to develop business in a legal marketplace that has grown increasingly competitive over the past several years. Particularly since the market downturn, clients are using in-house lawyers, consolidating work with fewer lawyers, and doing all they can to cut legal costs overall. As you become exposed to potential clients through your work, community activities, and networking efforts, you'll need to distinguish yourself from the competition and

---

[1] Aesop, *The Bat, the Birds and the Beasts*, in AESOP'S FABLES, http://www.aesopfables.com/cgi/aesop1.cgi?1& TheBattheBirdsandtheBeasts (last visited Nov. 17, 2012).

make yourself memorable. This process will be easier if you take the time to (1) develop some unique offerings and (2) learn to communicate about what you do in a way that is interesting and engaging to the people you meet.

### *Build a Unique Practice Within Your Practice*

### Finding a Niche

One of the best ways to distinguish yourself is to build a "niche practice." In this context, having a niche practice doesn't mean limiting your practice to one specialized area. Rather, it means building your skills, knowledge, and experience in a unique legal area so that you are one of the few "go-to" people in that area. A niche can be a subset of an existing substantive practice (e.g., animal trespass cases within the general area of real estate litigation), a geographic market sector (e.g., California water law), a demographic segment of the market (e.g., estate planning for retiring lawyers), or a combination of these (e.g., tax advice to American expatriates abroad).

Sometimes a niche may present itself because of a particular matter you worked on in which a unique issue arose that nobody knew how to handle. You may see e-mails going around your firm asking, "Does anybody know about XYZ law?," indicating that not many people have that expertise. Or a niche could arise from a passion or hobby of yours, for example, horse breeding transactions or wine law. Keep your eyes open for an area that is not adequately covered, for which there is a definite need, and about which you are interested in learning.

A niche is a handy marketing tool. It gives you a unique elevator pitch. It gives you a topic to speak about, allowing you to get out in front of groups. It provides potential for cross-referrals as you become the go-to person in your firm on that particular subject. And it gives you a topic to write about when you want to become more well-known.

Developing a niche is a relatively low-risk proposition. Particularly if you start in your associate years, you can accumulate knowledge over time and learn the niche area while you are still practicing primarily in a more general area of law.

## Defining the Market

Once you've chosen a niche, do some research to determine the likely demand for the service. If you've chosen elder law, for example, is the over-sixty demographic expected to grow in the next ten years? There are websites with statistics, social trends, and industry trends that can help you determine whether there is likely to be a growth in demand for the kind of service that you want to provide.

## Putting Out the Word

Once you've chosen your niche and determined that it's worth pursuing, start letting people know that you're an expert.

First, within your firm, see if you can give a presentation on the topic. This is a great way to both (a) market yourself internally and (b) practice giving presentations in your niche area. Once your colleagues know of your expertise, they can keep you in mind when their clients have a problem related to your niche area.

In addition to spreading the word internally, consider notifying existing clients of the firm of your new specialty. If you have a marketing department, the department can send a client update or press release. If not, you can talk with practice group leaders to see if they will spread the word to their clients. Focus particularly on those groups with which your practice is likely to have an affinity.

Finally, look for groups of lawyers who practice in your niche area but don't necessarily compete with you. They can be a great resource: a place to bounce ideas, to get marketing tips, and to keep up with developments in the niche practice area.

### Communicate Your Strengths and Uniqueness

You can be the greatest lawyer in the world with a tremendous amount to offer clients, but if nobody knows about your value, it won't do you much good. You need to learn how to communicate, both inside and outside your firm, those things that make you special (not only your niche but also other strengths and ways in which you are unique). This is where self-promotion comes in.

Most lawyers would rather have a root canal than spend time on self-promotion. Yet, it's one of the most important skills to learn if you want to boost your career. The product that you offer internally to your colleagues and externally to clients—including your talent, your credibility, and your image—can only serve people if they know about it. And people can't tell others how great you are unless they know it first.

Self-promotion does not mean fabrication, out-of-context pronouncements about how great you are, or putting down other people. Rather, it means taking a proactive approach to managing your career and communicating authentically the great things that you have done, are doing right now, and are capable of doing in the future.

### But My Work Will Speak for Itself . . .

Many people shun responsibility for self-promotion by telling themselves, "If my work is really good, it will speak for itself. I don't need to make a big deal out of it." People feel that bragging is unseemly; and rather than proactively communicating about their accomplishments, they leave to chance whether others will recognize them. This is a mistake.

You need to gain visibility, both inside and outside the firm. Once you take advantage of opportunities to promote yourself, people will learn what you do and remember your qualities when they need someone to help them.

In truth, self-promotion is a form of advocacy, something with which most lawyers are very comfortable. For example, suppose you have a client who was wrongfully accused of not paying a parking ticket. You have a copy of the check that she wrote to pay the ticket, with the citation number written on it. Everything is order. Would you mail that copy to the judge and assume that the clerk or the judge will make note of this fact? Would you send the ticket in and assume that the document will speak for itself, the clerk will deliver it to the judge, and the judge will notice it and take the initiative to dismiss the client's traffic case? No. You would appear in person on the appointed court date or before, with a copy of the ticket, and expressly tell the judge, "Here is Exhibit

A. It was written the day before payment was due. It was cashed by the clerk of the court, and it proves that my client paid her ticket." You would not leave it to chance; you would advocate for your client by highlighting the facts that establish her case.

The same is true for self-promotion. You need to advocate for yourself by highlighting accomplishments that demonstrate your competence. You can't leave to chance that you will be recognized, in part because your internal and external clients are constantly bombarded with information and in part because your competitors are advocating for *themselves*. If you don't promote yourself, you will fall behind.

## Identify Your Accomplishments and Keep Them in Mind

Effective self-promotion originates with knowing who you are and what you have to offer. The better you know yourself, the more authentic you will be in your relationships and communications. The more authentic you are, the more people will be drawn to you and the more success you will have. Once you know what you have to offer, you can "package" it in small sound bites that you can use when the opportunity presents itself.

Start by assessing your many accomplishments. Many people unconsciously minimize their successes and deflect compliments because they don't want to seem boastful. You need to consciously reverse that process by bringing to mind all of the great things that you can do and have done. In her book *Brag! The Art of Tooting Your Own Horn Without Blowing It,* author Peggy Klaus provides an excellent "Take 12 Self-Evaluation" for this purpose, which includes questions like these:

- What are the three most interesting things that you have done or that have happened to you?

- How did you end up becoming a lawyer?

- What career successes are you most proud of having accomplished (from your current position and past jobs)?

- What new skills have you learned in the last year?

- What professional organizations are you associated with, and in what ways—member, board, treasurer, or other position?

- How do you spend your time outside of work, including hobbies, interests, sports, family, and volunteer activities?[2]

Compose thoughtful answers to these questions, and then condense them into sound bites. For example, assume that one of the most interesting things you've done is to climb Mount McKinley. If the topic of vacations comes up, you might use a sound bite that sounds something like this: "I used all of my vacation time last year climbing Mount McKinley, but I'm not sure how relaxing it was. It took six months of training, and we had about four mishaps on the climb itself. I needed a vacation after the vacation." The sound bite should communicate your accomplishment, but in an anecdotal, humble way.

Presenting an interesting sound bite not only conveys your accomplishments but also keeps the conversation going. How many people might answer the question "Did you take any vacation last year?" by saying, "Yes, we went to Hawaii." Although this isn't a conversation killer, the mountain climbing sound bite, in contrast, gives the other person in the conversation the opportunity to ask follow-up questions, such as "What kind of training did it take?" or "What were the challenges you faced?" Those conversations make you memorable.

What if you didn't climb Mount McKinley? Then draw on other interesting experiences you've had that you can highlight at your networking events.

A related note: For purposes of making yourself memorable in conversations, it's also important to stay informed about current events. Read the newspaper each day and note two to three things you find interesting that you could bring up in a conversation in the next few days.

---

[2] PEGGY KLAUS, BRAG! THE ART OF TOOTING YOUR OWN HORN WITHOUT BLOWING IT 23–24 (2003).

**Prepare Your Elevator Pitch**

Your elevator pitch is an essential tool for communicating your value proposition. Once composed, you can lengthen, shorten, update, or edit it any way you desire in order to keep it fresh and relevant. But start with the basics. Create a ten-second speech that you can give smoothly, expressively, and automatically when called for by the situation.

To create a basic elevator pitch for a general audience as a response to the question "What do you do?," fill in the blanks in the form below:

I help _____ [**who are your clients?**] to _____ [**accomplish what goals or solve what problems?**] by _____ [**doing what to help them?**].

This is not as easy as it looks. Give yourself plenty of time to brainstorm different ways to fill in these blanks (and make sure that you pick a compelling verb when filling in the last blank—do not use *representing* or *advising*.) Remember that you don't need to describe your entire practice—just pick some attention-getting aspect. The goal is not to comprehensively disclose everything that you can possibly do for a client but to get the person you are talking to interested enough to ask more questions about your work.

Here are some examples:

- "I help **pharmaceutical companies** to **get their products to market** by **helping the FDA to understand their benefits.**"

- "I help **developers** to **build shopping centers** by **navigating the regulatory waters to get them the approval that they need.**"

- "I help **construction companies** to **get paid for their work** by **negotiating and enforcing their contracts with owners.**"

This is by no means an inflexible model; it's just a way to structure your thinking as you brainstorm your elevator pitch. There are no hard-and-fast rules for constructing this statement. The main goal is to communicate positively, in an interesting manner, the way in which your work benefits your clients. In other words, you shouldn't merely say, "I'm a bond lawyer" or "I'm a commercial litigator." By making these types of bland statements, you don't give the listener much to grab onto or ask more about, you risk losing your audience, and you waste a potentially valuable opportunity to make yourself memorable.

Once you've created your ten-second elevator pitch, practice it until you are comfortable. Go to events, and look for opportunities to use it. Share it with your partner or a close friend, and seek feedback on how it comes across.

After you are comfortable with your elevator pitch, tailor it to the situation. Through trial and error, you'll find out which versions work best in different settings and which elements trigger the best responses. In particular, you should create an expanded version, around forty-five to sixty seconds long. In contrast to the ten-second pitch, which is appropriate when you have very little time or are speaking to a casual listener, use the longer version to provide more detail when the person to whom you are talking is also a lawyer or has specifically asked you to say more about the kind of work that you do. In this version, you can include more about your experience and background:

> I represent pharmaceutical companies in the FDA approval process. I specialize in antidepressant drugs, which I studied intensively when I got my masters in biochemistry. The approval process typically takes three times longer for those drugs than any other FDA-reviewed products being produced right now because there's been so much litigation in the past ten years about three of the major antidepressant ingredients.

## Create Opportunities to Communicate Your Accomplishments

After you've given some thought to your accomplishments, or as new ones arise, look for natural opportunities to discuss them. For example, when you've successfully completed a project that others know about or were involved in at an early stage, take the opportunity to "close the loop" and send them an e-mail about it. When someone asks you what you're working on, don't waste the opportunity by saying "Not much" or giving some equally bland response; say something interesting about a project you're working on. If you are engaged in a long-term project for someone, send him periodic updates about what's been accomplished so far, without being asked. And look for opportunities to give credit to others whenever possible. People appreciate recognition, and when you have "tooted someone else's horn" in front of others, that person will be likely to return the favor someday.

# CHAPTER NINE

# Put Yourself Out There: Networking and Visibility

*"Out of sight, out of mind."*

One of the biggest transitions that you will need to make when you move from associate to partner is shifting your focus from internal to external. Although it's important in your early years to build clientele among the partners and gain a strong reputation for good work, a good attitude, and trustworthiness, you'll need to expand your reach and network to succeed as a partner. In chapter 7, we explained why relationships is so important, but in this chapter, the focus is on *how* to nurture relationships outside the firm and in particular make the most of networking events.

### The Networking Process

Networking is a habit to cultivate over your entire career; it's not a one-time experiment. You may nurture a relationship for many years that never leads to a piece of work, a referral to a resource, a job, or any tangible return on the investment. Accept that fact. The nature of networking is that you develop a network, build relationships, and maintain contacts. Over time, you will gain stature and credibility.

Your contacts are likely to grow and expand their opportunities as well. They will have struggles and victories. Your goal should be to actively support the people in your network, helping them in any way that you can, just as you hope they will support you.

### Create and Maintain a Contact List

The first step to effective networking is to create a list of your professional contacts. There are many software programs to facilitate this process, but one that is integrated with a calendar, such as Outlook, is easiest to use. Include your law school classmates, friends from college who are now in the professional community, and people you meet in the course of your practice. In addition to their names, addresses, e-mails, and telephone numbers, include information about their hobbies, interests, or any fact about them that makes them unique.

### Build Networking into Your Schedule

Schedule a regular weekly time to review your contact list and create communications with your contacts. Add any new contacts you've met and remove any old contacts you're not likely to interact with again. Select ten to twelve "top contacts" with whom you want to keep in touch. For each of those people, make a recurring calendar entry for an appropriate time period (for example, every ninety days for two years) to remind you to communicate with that person.

### Communicate with Your Contacts

The way in which you communicate with a particular contact will depend in part on who the person is, the nature of the relationship, and how well you know that person. If you've known the person for a long time or have a specific topic to talk to him about, schedule a lunch. If you don't know him as well, invite him to coffee. If the person isn't located close to your office or you don't know him well enough to ask him to coffee, send him an article of interest or comment on a recent news development that relates to him or ask him a question about his area of expertise.

When you are with the contact, think about the image you're projecting. Are you conveying a positive attitude? Think about how this person would view you someday if he wanted to hire you as his lawyer. Don't do, say, or wear anything that would make it hard for him to envision that. That doesn't mean you have to be phony—just be at your best, and remember that people will store information about you for a long time.

If it's a relatively new contact, send a note after the meeting thanking him for taking the time to talk. If you had an enjoyable conversation about a common interest or hobby, invite the person to meet again just to continue the conversation. If you identified some way in which you could help the contact, consider suggesting a follow-up meeting. The key is to build on each opportunity for contact and to learn as much as you can about the person so that you can identify ways to help him. This could take any number of forms: a job opportunity that you find out about and pass on; a board position that you suggest for him; information about an event that he would want to know about; or an invitation to a party he'd like to attend. There are no limits to the ways in which you can help your contacts. As you continue to stay in touch, many of your contacts are likely to become your business friends, and eventually some of your business friends may become close personal friends. Approach each person with an open mind, not wondering what he can do for you but asking yourself, "What can I do for him?"

## Use Social Media Wisely

Social media, particularly LinkedIn, can be a great way to increase and maintain visibility with your contacts. Update your profile by adding any new accomplishments, and revise your description of your practice area to make it more interesting. Make sure that there are no typos in any of your text. Send a brief status message when you attend an interesting conference, read a particularly helpful book, or complete a notable piece of work. Remember that your messages will have much greater impact if you limit them. Only send when you have something significant to say.

With all social media, of course, make sure that all of the information you project is positive and appropriate. Make sure that your Facebook page is free of incriminating photos and that there aren't any YouTube videos of you doing Jell-O shots.

*Making the Most of Networking Events: A Step-by-Step Guide*

Networking events serve at least two overlapping purposes. First, they create an opportunity to meet new people. Second, they provide an occasion for you to strengthen existing relationships and remind people that you're out there. The adage "out of sight, out of mind" is true, particularly for those in a position to hire lawyers because they are constantly bombarded by client alerts, lunch invitations, "helpful" articles, and other communications from lawyers eager to get their business. Staying visible will require an ongoing dedication of time throughout your career—it's a marathon, not a sprint.

Although you should make a point of attending events regularly, be selective about the kinds of events you attend. Attend events with a purpose in mind, knowing whom you want to meet or speak with when you're there. Attend events that will be attended by people to whom you want to talk. This would seem obvious, but it's surprising how many times lawyers attend a function without thinking about why they are attending. Of course, younger lawyers may have fewer choices than their senior colleagues and should thus be less selective, attending as many events as their schedules will allow; later, they can narrow down the events.

Attending an event as a newer lawyer, particularly one where you don't know many people, can be stressful. A little preparation and a plan of action will make it easier. Once you've followed the routine a few times, you'll get more comfortable and won't have to think about what to do next.

## Before the Event

To get the most out of a networking event, both in terms of enjoyment and expanding your network, make a plan before you go.

(1) *Research the event.* Find out what it's about, why it's being held, and who is likely to attend. If you have marketing assistance at your firm, staff members can often obtain a guest list for a local event. If not, you can call the organizer.

(2) *Set a goal.* Once you know what's going on, identify at least three people to whom you'd like to talk at the event, other than those you already know. If you have absolutely no idea who will be there, set a goal to meet a certain number of people.

(3) *Prepare for conversation.* Be sure to read the newspaper or an e-mail digest the day of or the day before the event. Make note of a few interesting items to comment upon, staying away from controversial subjects. If there will be a speaker at the event, research that person and think of a few questions to ask her. If the event is about a cause or a celebration, learn something about it and be prepared to discuss it.

(4) *Prepare your introductory and personal update information.* At any event that you attend, there are certain perfunctory conversations that are virtually guaranteed to take place. You can either recite boring responses to the general conversation-starter questions that you will be asked, missing an opportunity to spark further conversation and make yourself memorable, or prepare for these questions and make your responses more interesting:

- *"What do you do for a living?"* Be prepared to give your elevator pitch, as discussed in the previous chapter.

- *"What have you been up to?"* or *"What's new?"* Don't say, "Not much." Instead, say, "I just got back from a weekend in New York, and I saw the most amazing play" or "I just read an incredible book" or "We're still recovering from that huge hailstorm last weekend. It tore down one of our trees."

- *"What are you working on these days?"* Think of an example of something you're doing that is interesting and challenging and shows that you enjoy your work. Of course, never reveal confidential information about a client. Speak in general terms, e.g., "I'm working on a case where gold mining caused an environmental disaster and everyone who had anything to do with the site is being sued."

(5) *Get your business cards ready.* Keep your cards in one of your pockets, and designate another pocket for receiving cards from others. Be sure to have a pen readily available in the "outgoing cards" pocket so that you can make notes on your cards before giving them out. Don't make the mistake of attending an event without a business card. It never fails that the time you forget to restock will be the time you meet a VIP who's fascinated by what you do and wants to call you for a follow-up conversation.

## At the Event

(1) *Wear your name tag, if given one.* Give the people you meet the opportunity to learn your name, and the people you've already met the ability to remember it. Put it close to your right shoulder rather than your left. This is where people automatically look as they shake your hand.

(2) *Scan the room.* Observe the group formations. How many people are grouped together? Which ones are wrapped up in intense conversations? Do you see the key people with whom you wanted to speak? Is there anybody you know?

(3) *Approach.* There is no one-size-fits-all rule about whom to approach at every event, and no right answer for every situation.

- As a general rule, if there is a speaker at the event to whom you'd like to talk and she is accessible, talk to her before she speaks, if at all possible. In most cases, it will be much more difficult to get her attention after she speaks, and there may be a line of people waiting to do the same thing.

- If there is no speaker or if the speaker is not available, seek out people you know. Although it's definitely not a good idea to cling to people you know throughout an entire event, conversing with them is a great way to warm up and get yourself comfortable. It's especially helpful if they're in a group and can introduce you to others.

- Look at body language. Avoid groups of two, particularly if they look intensely engaged in conversation that may be private.

- Look for people alone. They are easy to approach and often grateful that you took the initiative to talk with them. In addition, you can often have a better-quality conversation in a one-on-one situation than you can in a group.

(4) *Engage.* If others are talking, listen carefully before you speak. Pick up the flow of the conversation; and when you have something to contribute, join in. With an individual you don't know, break the ice with easy questions such as "Have you been to this event before?" or "How long have you been involved with this organization"? As the conversation progresses, ask more open-ended questions. Listen carefully, and show you are actively listening by asking follow-up questions and affirming what the other person is saying.

- Do not talk about yourself until specifically asked. It's an amazing phenomenon that people often find most interesting those who are great listeners, not those who talk on and on about themselves. If you are talking in a group with a friend or associate, look for an opportunity to give your friend a "plug," or compliment an achievement of his when it fits into the conversation. The main rule to keep in mind is to ask more questions than you answer and listen more than you talk.

- Do not interrupt two people who look intently engaged in conversation, particularly if they are somewhat segregated from the crowd. Often, serious business gets discussed at events, and your interruption can be extremely annoying. If there is someone with whom you very much want to speak who is engaged in intense conversation with one other person, keep an eye out and wait for them to disengage. If that doesn't occur within a reasonable time or if you are unsure, go and stand near the two people whose conversation you want to join. If they keep talking and the conversation appears casual, look for an opening to join. If they stop abruptly and look at you, that means the conversation is not for you to join. Politely say hello to the person with whom you wanted to speak and tell him that you'll catch him later. You now have a reason to contact him after the event, and you can say, "I wanted to speak with you about X at the event last week but didn't want to interrupt you. Could we meet for coffee?"

- Give your FULL ATTENTION to the person with whom you are speaking. Even though there may be others you are looking for at the event and you are anxious not to miss anyone, it is extremely rude to keep glancing past someone when he is talking to you. Even if you only talk to someone for one minute, for that minute treat the person as though he were the most important person in the world. Listen to him intently and look at him. Bill Clinton was a master of this skill. He could win people over by listening, focusing, and convincing them that he cared about what they had to say. You can, too.

(5) *Move on.* Once the conversation reaches a lull, move on. Don't move on so quickly that you look overly eager to meet everyone in the room; but at networking events, people don't expect you to talk to them for the entire duration of the function. After ten minutes or so, excuse yourself and find someone else to approach and engage. Leave the other person wanting more from you, not tired of you. Ask for the other person's card so that you can contact him to continue the conversation if it's been particularly relevant or interesting. Offer your card if the other person asks for it or if it makes sense in the context of the conversation. Don't offer your card if you had no meaningful dialogue and didn't establish any reason for further contact.

(6) *Get food.* At some point, get food, particularly if it's served at stations or tables. These are gathering places, good places to meet and talk to others as you put food on your plate. Remember to eat only bite-sized food that doesn't interfere with your ability to converse and doesn't make a mess.

(7) *Relay thanks.* Before leaving the event, if at all possible, find the host, organizer, or member of the organizing committee. Compliment her on the event and thank her for the invitation.

(8) *Take advantage of your final opportunity.* As you leave the event, note the business cards that you've received. Was there anyone else you wanted to get a card from? Now is the time to go back and ask. Now is also a good time to write notes on the cards of people you met in order to help you remember them, e.g., "loves to ski" or "has eight children."

## After the Event

(1) *Update your contact list.* After you return to your office, add all business card information to your contacts list.

(2) *Add to your calendar entries.* Calendar dates and possible ways to follow up for each contact, such as providing information on a topic in which the contact expressed interest or just inviting the contact to coffee or lunch.

(3) *Connect via social media.* Check to see if the new contacts are on LinkedIn; if so, invite them into your network.

### Maintaining Visibility

In the business world, "out of sight" unfortunately often means "out of mind." In order to build your profile and maintain your network, it's important to be seen by your contacts periodically, whether individually or at events. Don't neglect to maintain visibility within your firm as well: attend firm functions, informal happy hours, and any other get-together to which you are invited. Showing up demonstrates that you care about the firm and your coworkers. Although sometimes you'll be extremely busy and would rather skip an event, try to avoid doing this if at all possible. Instead, show up for at least a short time. The organizer will appreciate it, and it's one more chance to be noticed.

Be proactive in maintaining visibility—don't just wait for invitations. Invite others in your firm to lunches, coffees, and happy hours. Don't limit your invitations to other lawyers, either: take the initiative to have lunch with your secretary or paralegal from time to time. Circulate within the firm as well. If you have to, set reminders to yourself to go visit other lawyers, particularly if your firm is on multiple floors of a building; it's easy to go for long periods of time without seeing people with whom we don't work directly. Make an effort to walk the halls periodically and drop in on your colleagues, even if just to say hello or ask how things are going.

You also have to think about how to increase your visibility in your later years as an associate, both inside and outside the firm. You do this by joining, getting active. Boards are great, but you actually have to serve on them. As discussed above, it's a huge mistake and a discredit to your personal brand if you join a board or commit to a volunteer activity in order to increase your visibility but fail to follow through. Failing to follow through is worse than if you hadn't joined at all.

## Writing

One way to maintain visibility is by writing periodically on a legal topic that you know about. It doesn't need to be a treatise or a law review article; in fact, to the contrary, it should be a short, succinct article on a topic that is timely and relevant to an audience of potential clients and referral sources whom you want to reach. If you've developed a niche, something not everyone knows about, you have a head start on finding a topic to write about. If you just completed work for a client involving a novel legal issue, you can use the research and knowledge you gained from that experience to write an article.

In addition to maintaining your visibility, writing articles serves many purposes. First, it builds your credibility in the legal or business community and can ultimately result in referrals of business because you're perceived as an expert in a particular area. Second, it builds your reputation within the firm and helps to reinforce the firm's reputation. Third, it improves your writing.

Professional journals are one possible avenue. Although an article in one of these may not be seen by prospective clients, it may be seen by other lawyers who are in a position to refer business to you. Such journals have a higher degree of credibility than some trade journals and help to establish you as an expert in your field. And if potential clients don't read the article initially, you can send it to them to add to your credibility.

## Speaking

Closely related to writing, and an excellent way to maintain visibility, is speaking at meetings, conferences, or other events where people want to hear what you have to say. Don't discount speaking at a bar association conference because, again, the idea is to establish yourself as an expert, get your face out there, and refine your oral communication skills.

One way to get more mileage out of your expertise is to write an article first and then turn it into a presentation. Once you have a presentation prepared, it's easy to modify it and give it several times. Try it the first time within your firm, and get some feedback. Over time, you'll build a collection of presentations that you can adapt and give on a moment's notice.

## Client Correspondence

Many lawyers don't take advantage of the opportunity to stay visible by corresponding with clients. Some firms prepare client alerts or advisories, small articles on hot legal topics that are sent to the firm's clients.

Sometimes, though, it can be more effective to send a personal letter to a selected client, potential client, or referral source, enclosing an article that is likely to be of particular interest to that person. If a client alert is written by a colleague of yours at the firm, consider enclosing it in a personal letter or e-mail rather than just directing the firm to send the alert to the client. Use the cover letter to reconnect with the client, mention something positive about your representation in the past, and introduce the topic contained in the client alert. This is a much more personal approach. Clients, particularly corporate in-house counsel, are bombarded with impersonal client alert e-mails and snail mail constantly. They will appreciate the personal touch. Letting them know that you're thinking about them is likely to be more important than the information in the article or client alert itself.

### The Desired Result

What is the end game of all this self-promoting, circulating, offering favors and information, and continuing to be seen? At some point, the stars will align. A contact with a need for legal help will remember you after you have built your credibility as a lawyer and done helpful things for that contact so that he will want to reciprocate.

# CHAPTER TEN

# Get the Business

*A Crow, half-dead with thirst, came upon a Pitcher which had once been full of water; but when the Crow put its beak into the mouth of the Pitcher he found that only very little water was left in it, and that he could not reach far enough down to get at it. He tried, and he tried, but at last had to give up in despair. Then a thought came to him, and he took a pebble and dropped it into the Pitcher. Then he took another pebble and dropped it into the Pitcher. Then he took another pebble and dropped that into the Pitcher. Then he took another pebble and dropped it into the Pitcher. Then he took another pebble and dropped it into the Pitcher. Then he took another pebble and dropped it into the Pitcher. At last, at last, he saw the water mount up near him, and after casting in a few more pebbles he was able to quench his thirst and save his life.*

*Little by little does the trick.*

*—Aesop*[1]

Developing business is a long-term process. Although theoretically it is possible to go to an event, meet someone with a legal problem, hand out your business card, and get a call the next day, most of the time a piece of business will result from a long series of contacts with someone in your network, sometimes over many years. That's why it's so important to start this process, and the habits embedded within it, early in

---

[1] Aesop, *The Crow and the Pitcher, in* AESOP'S FABLES, http://www.aesopfables.com/cgi/aesop1.cgi?sel&TheCrowandthePitcher2 (last visited Nov. 23, 2012).

your career. Every hour you spend is an investment in your ultimate success as a rainmaker. As a senior associate suggested:

> As an associate, you need to think ahead and ask yourself, 'Where will my business come from when I'm a partner?' Understand what it takes to build a book of business in your practice area. There is no standard way of developing business that applies to all areas. What works for corporate lawyers, whose clients may have a number of transactions over a period of years, may not work for bankruptcy lawyers or litigators, whose clients don't have as much repeat business.

Talk to senior lawyers in your practice group about how they initially built their book of business, what approaches worked, and what didn't work. Although even within your practice area someone else's method may not work for you, gathering information from several partners about developing business will give you an array of strategies to try yourself until you find what works for you.

### Rainmaking as an Associate

If you bring in work as an associate, it's likely you'll have to start with small matters. Don't worry; make the most of the experience and build on it for the future. The stature of the work that you are able to bring in will generally be proportional to your seniority in the practice of law and, correspondingly, the seniority of your peers. Clients tend to give work to attorneys of a similar age. Although this means that your rainmaking ability as an associate is limited, if you nurture your relationships from your early years of practice until the golden rainmaking years of thirty-five to forty-five, your peers will eventually direct business to you. You'll also have the ability to refer business to your peers and connect contacts who can benefit from knowing each other, which will benefit you because these peers and contacts will undoubtedly reciprocate.

A word of caution: Depending on how specialized you want your area of practice to be and the size of your firm, it's generally not a good idea to focus on bringing in business too early in your career. During your first three years, it's essential that you build your skills and focus on becoming a solid lawyer. In years four to six, you may be able to bring in some small matters, but that should not be your primary focus because the kind of work you're likely to bring in as a junior associate will probably not be complex or challenging. Though it seems counterintuitive, you may do a disservice to yourself and limit your experience by spending too much time on work for your own clients that is relatively simple and/or unrelated to your core practice area: you would be better served by working on more complex matters with senior lawyers for their clients until you have mastered the ability to handle more complex matters on your own. Of course, in a small or solo practice, you may not have a choice—you may need to take whatever you can bring in the door. But if possible, be strategic in allocating your time to matters that will benefit your growth in the long run instead of easy matters that will merely keep you busy in the short run.

### Not Shooting Yourself in the Foot

Picture this scenario: You've laid the foundation for business by building strong relationships throughout the legal and professional communities. You've created a practice niche that makes you the go-to person on a particular type of legal problem, in addition to your broader, established expertise in your chosen practice area. You've been attending events, staying visible, and promoting yourself by sending positive (yet tasteful) messages about your accomplishments. At some point, the stars align, and a potential client contacts you. How do you close the deal? This is the point at which, unfortunately, some lawyers shoot themselves in the foot. The business is ready to drop in their lap, but they blow it. There are several things that you should NOT do when a client opportunity knocks.

### Don't Be "Too Busy"

Don't tell a potential client that you're too busy to handle the work right now, assuming that he'll call you again in the future. Wrong! It's likely that he won't call you again. He will remember that you were unavailable in his time of need. There are always other good lawyers dying to get business. If you say no the first time you're asked, you've just given the competition a golden opportunity to rescue the client. You may never get another chance to get that business.

### Don't Claim Inexperience

Don't tell the client that his problem is not your area of expertise and leave it at that. Yes, you may be relatively inexperienced. Yes, the client may ask for help in an area that you don't know very well. WAIT a moment before you turn down the client. Keep in mind that clients don't like to hear "I can't do it" as an answer. Like the situation above, that client may never give you another chance. If you're in a firm, there may be another lawyer who has the expertise you need in order to serve the client. Lawyers team up with their partners all the time (or should, if they don't) to serve clients. Even if you can't do all of the work on the new client matter, you can win business for your firm and start a long-term relationship with that client. Eventually, the client may need exactly the kind of work that you do—or not. Regardless, don't automatically turn down the work just because you can't do it alone. If you investigate and it turns out that there is no one in your firm who has the necessary expertise, find another lawyer in your network who does have the expertise and who has a good reputation. At the very least, you'll receive the gratitude of the lawyer who receives the referral, and he is likely to return the favor when presented with a potential client who needs *your* expertise.

### Don't Neglect to Respond in a Timely Fashion

Don't take a long time to return the prospective client's call or e-mail. Believe it or not, some lawyers don't respond to e-mails and calls promptly. When a prospective client wants to reach you, respond as quickly as possible no matter where you are. Remember that clients often call a lawyer when they have a crisis—they may not have a long time to wait for a return call. If you don't respond quickly, a prospective client may just go down the list to the next available lawyer. At the very least, if you are unable to return a call or e-mail for several hours because, for example, you're in trial, have your secretary call the client to (1) let the client know that you received his call or e-mail and will respond at a specific time when you are able and (2) find out any details regarding the inquiry in order to begin any procedures such as opening a file or gathering necessary information.

## Don't Ignore Personal Time with Clients

Don't miss an opportunity to spend time with the client, particularly if it's early in the relationship. Of course, you have a personal life. But one of the most important ways to build a client relationship is for you and the client to get to know each other as people, not just as lawyer and client. If your prospective client invites you to an event, by all means make every effort to attend. If you're invited by a colleague to spend time at an event or have dinner with a client, seize the opportunity. Although you can't spend 100 percent of your time on your career, particularly if you have a family, recognize those golden opportunities that will never come again.

One associate, newly assigned to a high-profile real estate deal, had an opportunity to watch a baseball game with his firm's managing partner, other members of the deal team, and the client in the firm's private box seats. The associate said no because his wife had planned a dinner party for that night. This decision had multiple consequences. It branded the associate as relatively uncommitted to his career; it showed the client that the associate didn't really care about building a relationship with him; and it showed the managing partner the associate wasn't necessarily a team player or very concerned about building a relationship with him either. Don't be that associate.

## Don't Discount Client Proposals

Don't listen briefly to the client's problem and proposed solution and tell him that his proposal won't work. Clients hate to hear that something "can't" be done. If the client proposes a plan or solution that won't work, think carefully before responding. Ask probing questions to try and understand the intent behind the client's proposal, why it's important to him, and what he really needs in order to be satisfied with the outcome. Then, if at all possible, include in your response an alternative proposal, e.g., "I'm not sure that we can build apartments on that site, but we can look at getting a zoning variance. Have you looked to see whether another site might work?" Do everything you can to avoid giving a flat-out no.

## Don't Show Off

Don't be condescending to the client. Early in a relationship, you may be tempted to show the client how smart you are, to rattle off legal principles and jargon, and to come across as though you know it all. Resist this temptation. The client may recognize that behind this type of behavior is often insecurity; rather than increasing the client's confidence in you, it may have the opposite effect.

# CHAPTER ELEVEN

# Nurture and Grow Client Relationships

*"A bird in the hand is worth two in the bush."*

Existing clients are the best starting point for developing business. Though it seems obvious, it can never be stressed enough. "When you're laying the groundwork for business development, start with the clients you know and the groups you are part of, and branch out from there," suggests one senior associate.

Keeping your clients happy is the best thing that you can do for your career. Happy clients keep giving you more business. Happy clients refer their friends and colleagues to you. Happy clients pay their bills. And happy clients rarely, if ever, sue for malpractice.

The most profitable business that a firm can develop is repeat business from an existing client. Business generated through exceptional client service doesn't require an expensive pitch, the completion of an elaborate response to a potential clients "Request for Proposal," or sleek brochures and materials. You don't have to devise intricate plans for getting your foot in the door—since you're already working for the client, your foot is already in the door. You don't have to have researchers gather exhaustive intelligence on the client because you've learned about the client through direct contact. In short, your best opportunity to develop new business is to deliver the best service you can possibly give to existing clients.

### *Importance of Direct Client Contact*

Some of your best opportunities to build partner-level skills will arise when you begin to engage in direct client contact. You'll not only do a better job on the work that you are assigned, you'll build valuable client relationships as well.

In your early years as a lawyer, most of your information and instructions will come from the partners with whom you're working. You probably won't get much direct client contact other than calling to request particular pieces of information or interviewing a witness at a client company. But after you become more experienced and can convey authentic confidence in your abilities, look for as many opportunities for direct client contact as you can find. As another senior associate suggested,

> [A]lways make an effort to get as much face time with a client as you can. You learn a lot of things you will never learn by sitting at your desk. When there's a new matter that I know I'll be working on at some point, I ask the partner if I can sit in on client meetings, without billing the time, so that I can hear all of the background information from the beginning and really understand the client's objectives and what we are trying to achieve. This has worked well for me.

In order to get these opportunities, however, remember that you need to build trust with the partners for whom you work. A partner needs to know that you're not trying to steal his client by participating in the meetings, and he needs to know that you'll help him look good to the client, not hurt the relationship. Assure the partner that with direct client involvement, you'll be able to do a better job on the case or deal, and it will make his life easier. If you can get information directly from the client or have heard the entire background of the matter at a client meeting, you're less likely to have to keep bothering the partner with questions about particular issues.

In addition to seeking client contact on matters with which you're assisting a partner, ask for opportunities to handle a small matter on your own and serve as the primary client contact. When such opportunities are given to you, make the most of them.

As a young associate, you may not have friends who serve as general counsel at Fortune 500 companies. You may not have the opportunity to lecture at the local law school or play golf with the community's most prominent businesspeople. But when you have client contact on an active matter, you have the opportunity to bring in new business. Each client interaction is a chance to demonstrate your talent, grow the relationship, and increase the trust and respect that the client has for you and your firm.

An amazing number of associates fail to recognize the opportunity that comes from every contact with an existing client. They treat client interactions as just another part of the job, another task on the checklist to complete. In fact, they are much more. They are golden opportunities to build your client relations skills and engage in the most efficient business development activity there is.

### Inject Confidence in Client Contact

With direct client contact, there will no longer be a middleman between you and the client; you will become, for that interaction, the personification of the law firm to that client. Although it may seem intimidating at first, practice communicating in a calm, confident way. Practice listening well before you talk, doing everything you can to understand the situation before you make a suggestion or identify options. When you don't know the answer to a question, tell the client whatever you can that may be helpful, but admit that you will need to do some research in order to get the answer. Don't risk losing the client's trust by guessing an answer and getting it wrong.

You'll need to strike a balance between caution and confidence, however. If you lean too far toward the cautious side, refusing to state your opinion and appearing too wishy-washy, the client may feel that you're not on his side or, worse, that you aren't a capable lawyer. At least confirm for the client that you understand the question or the issue, and try to offer your point of view with qualifications, assuring him that you will confirm the answer and get back to him.

### Key Points of Client Contact

Every client relationship follows a certain course. Along this course, there are key points at which you have the opportunity to strengthen the relationship by providing quality experiences. A successful client relationship develops from an accumulation of these experiences. The critical points in the relationship include getting to know the client, getting to know the matter, setting expectations for the representation, keeping the client informed, making decisions, delivering good and bad news, billing, concluding the matter, and staying in touch.

### Getting to Know the Client

The first time you have the opportunity to work with a particular client, learn as much as you can about the individual you'll be dealing with and, if it's an institutional client, the history and nature of the organization. One of the most common complaints made by clients is that their lawyers never bothered to learn about them or, in particular, their business. Go to your first meeting with a good working knowledge of the client, and be prepared to ask intelligent questions that show you're thinking about his business. Ask clients if you can take a tour of their offices or facility so that you can better understand what they do.

Whether your representation is transactional or for litigation, you will almost always find it beneficial to learn about the client's business in order to place facts in context, identify the jargon used by the client, and understand some of the common challenges that your client faces. The more knowledge you have about clients, the better you will be able to serve them.

Particularly as a young lawyer, you have the opportunity to distinguish yourself by actively seeking to learn about the client. Often, more senior lawyers with an established book of business don't think about delving deeply into the client's business. They forget how impressed clients are when lawyers are curious about them.

Going to the client's facility also gives you a potential opportunity to meet more key players at the client company. Pay particular attention to individuals who are close to your age and years of professional seniority. These are the most promising individuals for you to build long-term relationships with: when they become decision makers, they'll look to you for their legal needs.

## Getting to Know the Matter

Each time you work with a particular client, you'll need to learn all you can about the matter on which you've been assigned to work. If it's a transaction, strive to understand what the client wants to achieve, what the key facts and issues are, and what role the client expects you to play. This may involve a combination of client meetings, phone calls, and review of documents. Keep in mind that the ability to define and resolve a client's problems can be just as important as technical legal skills.

Often, lawyers are so eager to show a client how much they know that they start offering possible solutions before they fully understand the problem. Your most important skills in face-to-face interactions with a client, particularly at the beginning of a new matter, will be listening and asking questions. Listen to everything the client says, and paraphrase periodically to confirm that you are correctly understanding the client. Ask open-ended questions that neither assume a specific answer nor limit the context that the client is trying to provide. By listening carefully, you show the client that you care and that you are invested in accomplishing his goals.

## Setting Expectations for the Representation

One of the most important phases of the attorney-client relationship is when, after gathering enough information to form a plan of action, the attorney sets the client's expectations for the process and eventual outcome. Such expectations include the following:

- how the process is likely to go

- how much the work is likely to cost, within certain parameters, including the hourly rates that will be charged, the amount of time it is likely to take, and other significant costs that are likely to be incurred

- what the attorney will do and, if relevant, what he will not do

- what the client is expected to do (this is very important, particularly in litigation when the client may be expected to produce documents, submit to depositions, answer written discovery requests, and the like)

- what problems or challenges they may encounter

- how often and by what means they will communicate about the matter

- any risks that may be inherent in the course of action

- how success will be measured at the end of the representation

As you set these expectations, if there are any troubling issues, discuss them with the client sooner rather than later. Many times, particularly with a new client relationship, attorneys underestimate some of the difficulties that may be encountered in meeting the client's objectives because they are eager to start off by creating a positive impression. Don't make that mistake. A realistic assessment up front will save the client from frustration and disappointment later and help preserve the client's trust in you.

Once the expectations are set, they must be managed on an ongoing basis. As events occur or facts develop that change the process, the plan, or the likely outcome, let the client know. Overcommunicating is always better than undercommunicating. Nothing erodes a client's trust more easily than hearing unexpectedly that something you projected hasn't turned out to be true.

This is particularly true with budgetary expectations. Attorneys often underestimate the problems they cause for corporate counsel, in particular, when legal fees exceed the amount projected. Attorneys forget that unlike law firms, most corporations operate on budgets. In-house counsel set budgets just as other functional leaders in a company do and are held accountable for meeting them. Help your client look good by staying within budget or, if you can't, notifying him as quickly as possible about the estimated overrun.

## Keeping the Client Informed

Once the expectations are set, agreements are made, and the representation is under way, keep the client informed of all material developments. Although sophisticated clients may specify a particular mode or frequency of reporting, most of the time it will be up to you to recognize events or developments that the client will want to know about. Particularly when you are first working with a client, err on the side of over-informing them rather than underinforming. If the client wants you to report less often or considers a particular type of development unimportant, he can let you know. Absent that, assume that the client will want to know about virtually anything that affects the representation.

Keeping a client informed is important for several reasons. First, it shows you are diligent and care about the client. Second, it helps build the relationship and create trust. Third, and perhaps most importantly, however, it reduces the likelihood of malpractice claims. Don't cause your client to feel mistreated or ignored. Stay in regular contact and provide all the information you reasonably can about the matter.

## Making Decisions

From time to time, you'll need to consult the client to make a particular decision affecting the representation, e.g., whether to hire an expert or other consultant, whether to take a particular position in negotiations, or whether to pursue a particular remedy that has emerged since the representation began. These are points in the representation when you can shine. Although some clients are more sophisticated than others and need more explanation or stronger guidance, all of them want good information on which to base a decision. Provide them with context, an accurate assessment of the options, the pros and cons of each option, and your recommendation. Then let the client choose.

Clients particularly resent having decisions imposed on them by their lawyers. If the client doesn't feel that it was his decision—in other words, if he doesn't feel that he "owns" the decision—you will certainly hear about it if the outcome is poor. Many lawyers feel that they have superior knowledge and are tempted to show a client how smart they are by paternalistically shoving a decision down the client's throat. Avoid this, and you will have a better chance of maintaining (and even increasing) the client's respect for you.

## Delivering Good and Bad News

Make a conscious effort to deliver news well, whether it's good or bad.

If a particularly positive development has occurred, call the client to let him know. Depending on the degree of the client's sophistication, tell him what could have happened and why the development is particularly beneficial for him. You don't have to brag about your own efforts or role in bringing about the results. Your client will know and will give you credit. Just make sure that the client understands when you've achieved something significant for him, particularly something that is greater than expected at the outset of the representation.

When you have bad news to deliver, don't avoid it or downplay it. Let the client know, and give your best explanation as to the likely reasons the result occurred. The client should never hear bad news from a court, opposing party, or newspaper first. Be straight with the client about what has happened, what (if any) options there are for dealing with it, and what you recommend as the next steps for going forward.

## Billing

The communication that occurs through your billing statements is one of the most critical points of client contact that you will have. Don't underestimate the importance of this document and what it means. Your billing statement, comprised of your detailed time entries, is what tells clients the value that you brought to them, i.e., the reason why they should pay you the thousands of dollars that you are charging. In addition to the tasks performed, a client learns a great deal by looking at a billing statement:

- *Did you follow directions?* Does the statement conform to any guidelines that the client provided at the beginning of the representation, or did you ignore them? Ignoring them is a great way to not get paid.

- *Were you attentive to details?* Your careful proofreading of the billing statement, which should be free of errors, tells the client that you were likely attentive to the details of his representation as well.

- *Did you try to keep costs down?* Your billing statement should show that you delegated work to the person who could do the job competently at the lowest cost.

- *Did you go beyond the call of duty, at no charge?* Depending on the matter, it can be advisable to add some bonus tasks to the bill, next to which you should indicate "no charge." Clients often appreciate the extra effort that doesn't cost them anything.

Pay careful attention to the information you put in your time entries and billing statements. These are not just administrative documents; they are the communication that "sells" the work that you have done and convinces the client of the value that you add.

## Concluding the Matter

Even if you think it's obvious that a matter is concluded, always send a closing letter to the client. Briefly describe the outcome, and highlight any particularly good results or unintended benefits that your client received in the course of the matter. In addition to the reasons described in chapter 13 for risk management purposes, sending a closing letter provides an opportunity to finish on a high note, highlight your accomplishments in the representation, and make yourself memorable to the client.

## Staying in Touch

The last key point of contact in the life of a representation is to reach out to the client later, even when nothing is pending.

After you've concluded a matter, calendar a date thirty to sixty days later on which you will call the client to check in. Prepare some questions to ask the client to find out how things are going, if the representation brought about the result that the client wanted, whether there were any unintended consequences, and whether any new or related work might be helpful. For example, after a client sued successfully to collect on a promissory note, are there other notes to consider litigating? After a client successfully acquired a smaller company, could there be more acquisitions on the horizon?

Then, set a date that makes sense, perhaps six months out, to contact the client just to check in and say hello. Look for an opportunity to call the client based on an interest that he has (e.g., "There's been particularly good snow for skiing this year") or based on a news story that made you think of him (e.g., "I saw that your company made the 'Best Places to Work List' this year-congratulations!"). Part of maintaining client relationships is reminding clients that you are out there. Although some clients may be contacts whom you encounter regularly, those that are not should receive a call now and then.

### *Client Relationships: Setting Yourself Apart*

Always keep in mind that there are (usually) many lawyers who can do what you do, have a comparable level of expertise and, from a legal skill standpoint, do the work as well as you can. What sets you apart is how the client feels about you as a person, the exceptional service you provide, and whether it's clear that you care about him.

Getting to know the client as an individual is key to establishing a long-term relationship. Once the client knows you and likes you, you can keep the client loyal by going the extra mile—thoroughly learning the client's business, fully understanding each matter, listening to the client's objectives and concerns, informing the client of all developments, delivering news tactfully, and keeping in touch when active matters are over. Maintaining a great relationship will distinguish you from every other lawyer, so pay as much attention to the relationship as you do to providing great service.

# CHAPTER TWELVE

# Get Work Done Through Others

*"Many hands make light Work."*

*"I get by with a little help from my friends."*

Lawyers are among the most autonomous and independent individuals in our society. Just as they resist the notion of being "managed" in the way that most companies manage their employees, they resist the notion that they must learn how to manage and supervise others in order to be successful.

One of the eternal dilemmas that many talented lawyers face is whether to sacrifice some degree of independence and control by working in a firm (where they have fewer administrative responsibilities, more staff support, and the potential to earn a higher income through leverage) or to maintain independence and control in a private practice (where they will sacrifice some efficiency, ready access to the expertise of others, and a greater potential for income). It's true that lawyers who practice entirely on their own can avoid having to manage staff members or junior attorneys; however, their success will be limited by their own expertise (having no partners available to fill in missing areas of expertise), their acumen as a business owner, and their capacity for billing hours after performing clerical and managerial tasks. In other words, it's difficult to practice effectively without at least *some* amount of staff support. And with staff comes the need to manage people.

There is only one of you. If your potential to service clients depends solely on the work that you can do in a day, a week, or a year, you are going to be limited in what you can accomplish and how much you can earn. The key to writing your own ticket is to be able to effectively delegate to others, manage teams, and teach others to manage teams. And the better you do it, the more successful your practice will be.

### Delegation Tips

People often underestimate the challenges of being a good delegator. They hand off an assignment with little explanation, get back a poor product, and blame the delegatee. Senior associates are notorious for complaining that partners aren't good delegators but then turn around and do the same thing to junior and summer associates. The following five steps will help you to delegate more effectively.

### Know Your People's Abilities

Take the time to talk to your assistants about the range of their capabilities and the functions they routinely handle. Have the same conversations with your paralegals and junior attorneys. Because capabilities, experience, and degrees of development differ among individuals with the same job title, don't assume that you know the potential and limitations of the person with whom you are working. Taking the time to ask will provide you with valuable information and possibly uncover resources that you didn't know you had available.

### Plan the Delegation

Before you contact the delegatee to make the assignment, take a few minutes to plan. Is the task one that's appropriate for delegation? What is the goal in terms of the product you want from the delegatee? What documents and other resources will the junior attorney need in order to do a good job? What deadlines are involved? Taking the time to plan can help you be clearer when you discuss the assignment with the delegatee.

After you analyze the task, think about who is the right person for the job. Is it an assistant or paralegal? A summer associate? A junior associate? Think outside the box, and don't limit yourself to always using the same individuals. Larger firms often have reference librarians who can help with research, word processing departments that can help with large document-creation jobs, and others who can help for an even lower billing rate than an associate or paralegal.

## Assign Clearly and Completely

When you delegate an assignment, try to meet with the delegatee in person or speak on the phone. This gives him a chance to ask questions and reflect back that he understands the assignment, and it helps you to confirm that you gave the instructions the way you intended. When you communicate the assignment, make sure you do the following:

- Provide context for the assignment that gives the delegatee the "big picture." This helps the delegatee feel like part of a larger, more important cause rather than just an employee doing a discrete assignment.

- Clearly describe the desired product you expect, i.e., a formal written document, a short outline, or an oral summary.

- Estimate the amount of time that you think the project will take. If it's a fairly lengthy assignment, have the delegatee check in after approximately one-third of the time has been used. That way, you can confirm that the project is proceeding at the pace you expected, and you can correct course if things are not on track.

- Tell the delegatee the deadline for completion so that there is no confusion about when you expect to receive the completed assignment.

- Ask for a recap of the assignment from the delegatee so that you can confirm his understanding of the assignment.

## Establish a Line of Communication

Depending on the complexity of the assignment, you may want to set interim check-ins so that you can confirm the project is on track. At a minimum, tell the delegatee how to reach you so he can ask questions as needed. Tell them your communication preferences, both in terms of mode of communication (phone, e-mail, in person) and time of day, if applicable. Staying available for communication is one of the best things you can do to help insure that you receive the result or work product you expect.

## Provide Honest Feedback

Finally, when the assignment is done, provide honest feedback on the work product in the most constructive and helpful manner possible. It serves no one if the delegatee doesn't hear what you liked and didn't like about the work, what met your expectations and what didn't. Avoiding this step will only make it more difficult in the future to get the product you want from this individual.

### Common Objections to Delegation

Lawyers sometimes resist delegating assignments when their hours are low and work is scarce. They keep the work for themselves, even though it's beneath the type of work expected at their billing rate. This is a mistake because it prevents junior attorneys and paralegals from performing to capacity, costs the client more than it should, or results in a write-off. It also distracts you from doing what you should be doing in that situation, which is looking for more work. Instead of keeping the work for yourself, delegate to others and spend the extra time developing business: contact internal clients first and let them know that you are available, get the word out to others that you are looking for work, network, attend events, and establish visibility in the community.

Another common objection to delegating is the old excuse "It's faster and easier to just do it myself." Yes, that may be true. But that is a shortsighted approach. The point is to teach others to do lower-level tasks so that you can focus on higher-level tasks. Each time you keep the work, you are depriving a junior person of an opportunity to learn and develop. Once you delegate a few times and provide adequate instruction, it won't be easier to do it yourself and you'll get the product that you want.

Remember that delegation is a long-term strategy, not just a quick fix when you're in a jam. You'll delegate, the person will make mistakes, you'll give feedback that helps the person learn to do it right, you'll delegate again, and there may still be some mistakes. Be patient. Don't expect perfection. And particularly with young associates, remember what it was like when you were new to the practice of law. It's a confusing time, and young lawyers need encouragement. In a few cases, you may encounter someone whose skills are truly subpar. But most of the time, perceived inadequacy is the delegator/supervisor's fault, and talent is unnecessarily thrown away.

### Delegation Styles

Similarly, keep in mind the experience level of the delegatee in deciding how specifically to give directions and how tightly to control the project. To a very junior lawyer, you may have to do training-type delegation, with a lot of detailed instructions and frequent check-ins along the way. With someone more experienced, you can let go of the reins a bit more, and give them some freedom to decide how to do the task.

With the most experienced associates and paralegals, on a project they've done many times, a "hands off" style is more appropriate. This means you give them the matter, they assume primary responsibility, but check with you on major decisions. Your degree of involvement depends on the nature of the matter and the experience level of the associate, but ideally you don't have to spend much time guiding this associate to do the client work.

### Sideways Delegation

At times, you may bring in work for a client or be asked to do work for an internal client for which you don't have all of the necessary expertise. If you are in a firm and can access others who do have the expertise, take advantage of this resource. Rather than keeping the work yourself and attempting to "learn as you go," take the opportunity to build an internal relationship. The degree to which you retain control may depend on the client relationship. At a minimum, if you hand off a matter to one of your partners, you should check in with both the client and the partner from time to time to see how things are progressing. Even if it's a client you haven't worked with before or don't know very well, the client may hold you responsible for the work of your partner. Don't assume that once you've passed the matter on, you have no responsibilities. Staying in touch with the client and working partner will help you identify and resolve any problems that may arise, help protect your reputation, and make it more likely that the client will come back to you when he has a matter that falls within your area of expertise.

In some cases, you may team up with your partner rather than delegating completely. This may give you a chance to learn a new area of law, if it's not too far afield from what you normally do, and also build a relationship with your partner. Alternatively, you may ask your partner to merely serve as a consultant on the matter, providing advice from time to time. Whatever the degree of control you decide to retain, be sure and communicate clearly with your partner and the client about who will be responsible for what.

### Supervision

Your responsibility for the work product doesn't end after you've delegated a particular project. You need to check in on the progress and provide substantive guidance, particularly for assignments that the associate doesn't know how to do very well. Many lawyers overlook this responsibility, which isn't only important for getting the job done right—it's important from an ethical perspective as well.

The degree of supervision required for a given matter will depend on several factors, including the experience level of the associate, the degree of complexity of the matter, and any particular preferences of the client for whom you are working. Particularly with a fairly junior associate, however, take the time to evaluate his work product. Many senior lawyers, particularly those who are used to working with experienced associates, forget how little junior associates know when they first begin to practice. Look carefully at a memo before you send it to the client. For a very new associate, you may even want to have a senior associate double-check some case citations to make sure that the cases stand for the propositions represented.

Not only must senior lawyers carefully review the product, they must take the time to explain mistakes to the junior lawyer. This step is often overlooked by busy lawyers, who simply rewrite a document themselves rather than sitting down with the associate to discuss the specific ways in which the document can be improved.

### More on Giving Feedback

Feedback is a skill that has been touched upon earlier in this chapter, but it is important enough to warrant its own section. Giving feedback is incredibly difficult for all people, but especially for lawyers. Feedback needs to be both formal and informal. The formal evaluation is intended to combine feedback from many projects over time and assess the overall progress of the associate within the firm. Informal feedback—the emphasis of this section—focuses on a particular piece of work and should be timely and specific.

Feedback must be timely in order to be understood and synthesized effectively. The longer you wait to deliver the feedback, the greater the risk that the associate will not understand or recall specifically what you are talking about. Delaying feedback also prevents the associate from absorbing it and changing his behavior right away. This is particularly true with annual evaluations: if the feedback wasn't given at the time of the assignment, it can be next to useless. The formal evaluation should never be the first time that an associate hears feedback or a particular trait or behavior.

Feedback must also be specific. General comments such as "Nice job" don't tell an associate what they did that they should repeat in the future. Was it a particularly concise piece of writing? Did the associate address exactly the issue you were concerned about? Similarly, comments such as "You don't have very good oral communication skills" don't tell an associate what he needs to work on in order to get better. Does he need to speak louder? With more confidence? After more careful preparation? Again, being specific will make it more likely that your feedback will make a difference and improve the associate's performance.

One method for giving feedback that is easy to use and widely accepted is the SBI (S=Situation, B=Behavior, I=Impact) method, advocated by the Center for Creative Leadership and other management experts:[1]

- *Situation.* What was the context in which the behavior occurred? At a particular negotiation meeting? On a conference call? In a particular memo?

- *Behavior.* Tell the associate what behavior you observed. For example, "Last week when you sent me your memo on piercing the corporate veil, I received it at 5:00 p.m. instead of 12:00 p.m., as we had discussed." Make sure the associate recognizes the situation and behavior you're talking about, so you are on the same page.

- *Impact.* Describe the impact that the associate's behavior had on your practice. For example, in the above scenario, the partner might say, "I had a client meeting at 1:00 p.m. because the client was going to go into a board meeting at 3:00 p.m. to discuss the piercing claim. Because I didn't have your memo at noon, I wasn't able to give her any guidance, and she looked foolish in front of her board of directors."

Ask the associate for his recommendation on how to handle a similar situation next time. By allowing the associate to recommend a corrective approach, you increase his level of buy-in and the likelihood that he will engage in that behavior in the future. Offer your own recommendation if the one suggested by the associate is unacceptable or needs clarification.

---

[1] *See generally* Sloan R. Weitzel, Feedback that Works: How to Build and Deliver your Message (CCL Press 2000).

Once you have gone through this process, confirm that the associate heard you by saying something like, "Does that make sense?" or "What was going on for you in that process?" Ultimately, make sure that you and the delegatee agree on what happened, why it was problematic, and what should happen in the future.

### Other People-Management Activities

"Managing" people involves many different processes, including selection as well as delegation and supervision. If you have an opportunity, join the firm's hiring or recruiting committee. Participating in the attorney hiring process can provide you with great insights on what attributes the firm's decision makers look for in lawyers whom they hire and promote. It also helps you develop a skill—evaluating talent—that you can use for the firm's benefit throughout your career. This skill will be valuable whether you serve on a committee that makes hiring decisions or merely participate in the process by interviewing potential candidates.

Orientation and integration are additional people-management areas in which partners can add value. New attorneys joining the firm, whether as first-year associates, lateral associates, or lateral partners, need assimilation into the firm in order to maximize their value. This can only happen if the lawyers already practicing in the firm take the time to get to know the new lawyers and show them around. Both informal efforts at reaching out to new lawyers and formal orientation programs help new lawyers develop a comfort level for practicing effectively, understand how to use the firm's resources for the benefit of their practice, and begin building relationships that foster teamwork and loyalty throughout the firm.

# CHAPTER THIRTEEN

# Go Beyond Delegation: Develop and Lead Others

*"A good leader inspires others with his confidence. A great leader inspires them with confidence in themselves."*

—*Reed Markham*

At a fairly early stage, as noted in the previous chapter, it will become apparent to you that you need to be able to leverage the help of others in order to build a successful practice within a law firm: you need the ability to delegate work to junior associates and staff in order to maximize your productivity. But as you prepare for a more meaningful role in the firm, you will need to think beyond just getting work done for your own clients and focus on the greater good of the firm as well. Developing the firm's talent is an important role that you will have as a partner. This implicates leadership skills that require a true concern for the firm's well-being and the emotional intelligence to influence a broad group of people.

Leadership means much more than just getting along well with others. Simply stated, leaders are those who bring out the best in those around them by inspiring them. The ability to lead will make you extremely valuable to your firm, help you make a difference in your community, and, ultimately, increase your demand by clients.

### Position Yourself for Leadership

As an associate, you are building a brand for yourself. Ideally, this brand will establish you as someone who does quality work, is dependable, goes beyond the call of duty, helps others, and has good judgment.

This brand will determine, to a large extent, the trust that the firm's leaders will be willing to place in you and consequently, the opportunities for leadership that you will be offered within the firm.

A surefire way to destroy that trust, or to prevent it from forming at all, is to become known as a complainer—someone who repeatedly criticizes the firm leaders' decisions. Even if you only intend to voice your gripes to a small group of colleagues, word will get out. "Keep your head down. Don't complain about things the firm does or what's happening to other associates. You can't fix it. You'll only hurt yourself by getting upset and complaining about it. You'll get a bad reputation, and you'll ruin your own peace of mind," advises Phil Gosch, a partner of Brownstein Hyatt Farber Schreck in Denver, CO. "Keep your head down and ignore the noise. Later, when you become a partner, you can do something about it."

In particular, complaining about how another associate has been treated (in your view) will serve no positive purpose for your career. Not only does this kind of negativity damage your perceived trustworthiness, but often the secondhand information on which you are basing the opinions is incomplete or distorted. This happens, for example, when associates voice criticism of the firm's treatment of another attorney who was asked to leave. For obvious reasons, the firm's leaders cannot disclose the performance or behavior reasons that prompted an employee's termination. Consequently, whatever gossip you hear in the grapevine about whether the attorney "deserved" it or not is inherently suspect, and may well have been disseminated to advance another complainer's own agenda. Stay neutral in these situations and try to give the firm the benefit of the doubt. Assume that there were good reasons for the decision, and leave it at that. Your reputation, trustworthiness, and overall sanity will fare far better if you avoid immersing yourself in personnel and management issues that have nothing to do with you.

### Develop the Firm's Talent

It's one thing to engage other lawyers in your practice out of necessity, to meet your clients' needs in a timely and cost-effective manner. But to build a successful practice, whether you are solo or in a firm, you have to go further and think longer term. You need to develop the lawyers who work for you and demonstrate leadership skills that benefit the firm as a whole, not just your practice directly.

Developing others means giving conscious thought to the assignments they are getting, providing helpful feedback on specific work, coaching them on career decisions, helping them navigate the firm, and encouraging them when they show signs of losing heart. It means looking beyond the immediate work they are doing and helping them build a successful career. It also means making an active effort to engage them in dialogue. Unfortunately, some more experienced lawyers don't take these opportunities or put thought into developing those whom they supervise.

The true leader will feel a sense of responsibility for developing and mentoring junior lawyers, both as an obligation to the profession and a responsibility to the firm. By passing along their knowledge, true leaders feel, in some small way, that their value will continue to live on even after they retired from the practice. Leadership means planting a seed, putting in effort to grow someone else—even though there may be no personal benefit in it. At the other end of the scale are those who, consciously or unconsciously, deprive subordinates of growth opportunities because they are insecure and afraid that the junior lawyer will outshine them or take clients away. To develop others is to let them shine and thrive, being confident enough in your own talents not to feel threatened. It means letting go of some control so that the younger lawyer can get experience even though he might make a mistake.

## In the Context of Assignments

Associates need, more than anything, the chance to develop and build their skills. Without this opportunity, their careers are at risk. Although training and mentoring make strong contributions to an associate's development, the two most critical components are (1) the work assignments they are given and (2) the quality of the supervision they receive while working on these assignments.

There are those who merely delegate and those who develop. Those who merely delegate give an assignment, perhaps some feedback, and essentially use the associate to get their work done without giving thought to how this work is contributing to the associate's long-term development as a professional. Those who develop make the time to sit down and talk with the junior lawyer periodically, taking advantage of teachable moments in the course of work on a case or matter (e.g., when an opposing counsel attempts to change a deal term after several drafts of an agreement have already been exchanged and discussed; a judge makes a ruling reflecting that she didn't understand one of the parties' arguments; or a client attempts to take a position that is contravened by its own documents).

Think about how you can challenge the junior lawyers who work for you. As you sense they are ready to take more responsibility, give them opportunities to stretch rather than the same repetitive tasks over and over. Give them a chance to try new techniques in a safe environment, where you will oversee their first few efforts at a particular type of task or activity.

When they are ready, give them responsibility for an entire client matter. This is one of the best ways for them to learn how to take ownership of an assignment and feel responsible for meeting the client's needs. Without a partner in the middle, the associate feels the direct connection to the client, has an opportunity to immerse himself in the matter at hand, and will often deliver a better work product than he would have delivered through a partner.

Finally, seek feedback after you've worked with a junior lawyer on several assignments to find out if your guidance has been helpful and whether there is anything *you* can improve about your style that could bring out the best in the lawyers you supervise.

### In the Role of Mentor

You can provide leadership to younger lawyers by serving as a mentor, whether through a formal program or informally. Although the roles of mentor and supervisor can overlap, a mentor is different from a supervisor in that mentors offer big-picture advice that goes beyond a particular assignment and, in fact, need not even work with the associate in order to provide valuable guidance. A lawyer often benefits from having multiple mentors who provide different types of help and different perspectives on the practice of law.

Take a junior lawyer with you to an important event in your practice, such as a hearing in court, the closing of a transaction, or a negotiation session. Let him sit in on your client phone calls without billing the client. Talk to him about his work—what he could have done better and what he did well—and his overall career path.

One of the most valuable things that you can do for your protégé is to help him build relationships, both inside and outside the firm. Introduce him to partners and associates in other practice groups, particularly those who serve important roles within the firm. Introduce him to people who can help him become involved in a particular organization. Include others when you take your protégé to lunch, coffee, or happy hour so that in a comfortable setting he can meet people he might not have met otherwise.

Don't forget about your protégé when you're not working with him. Drop by your protégé's office from time to time (put a recurring reminder on your calendar if you need to). Ask questions about what your protégé is working on and how things are going. Show concern by asking how you can help. A combination of scheduled meetings and activities and casual drop-ins will help form a trusting relationship, one that will allow your protégé to share real concerns and make real progress in advancing his career.

### In Positions of General Leadership Development

You can also help to develop the talent at your firm by completing formal performance evaluations even though they are time-consuming; by taking new associates to lunch and speaking with them at events in order to integrate them into the firm; by participating on committees that impact associate development; and by advocating policies that enhance the training, mentoring, work assignments, and feedback that the associates in your firm receive.

### *Be a Multiplier, Not a Diminisher*

It is assumed that experienced lawyers are smart, and therefore qualified to lead teams of junior lawyers. As a rule, however, lawyers do not study management and motivational techniques. Lawyers, who are specialists by nature, are highly focused on subject matter knowledge and legal analysis and may overlook the impact of their actions on others' feelings, attitudes, and morale. As a leader in your firm, though, you have a far greater ability to impact others than you realize.

At a fundamental level, as a leader, you have the opportunity to (a) make those around you smarter, more talented, and more capable; (b) have little or no impact on others; or (c) reduce the intelligence of those around you, sap their energy, and drain them of motivation. In their breakthrough book, *Multipliers: How the Best Leaders Make Everyone Smarter*, Liz Wiseman and Greg McKeown articulated with refreshing clarity how leaders who practice the disciplines of "Multipliers" bring out the best in those around them and accomplish amazing results with their teams. They do this by attracting talented people, using them at their highest point of contribution, and creating an environment that requires their best thinking; defining opportunities that cause their team members to stretch; driving sound decisions through rigorous debate; and giving other people ownership of the results they achieve.[1] In contrast, "Diminishers" hoard resources and underutilize talent; create a tense environment that suppresses people's thinking and capability; give directives that showcase how much they know; make centralized, abrupt decisions that confuse the organization; and drive results through their personal involvement.[2]

Unfortunately, some law firms tolerate abusive, disrespectful, and even at times dishonest behavior by partners who are significant rainmakers. This can lead to a toxic environment within the "diminishing" partner's practice group that can eventually spread to the entire firm. At first, the complaints come from associates. They are countered by the toxic partner, and the complaining associates are discredited. Eventually, more associates make similar claims, whether they involve sexual harassment, unfair criticism, insults, or other demoralizing behavior. Some partners start to notice that this is affecting their associates. They start

---

[1] LIZ WISEMAN & GREG MCKEOWN, MULTIPLIERS: HOW THE BEST LEADERS MAKE EVERYONE SMARTER 21–26 (HarperCollins 2010).

[2] *Id.*

to listen and argue that something should be done. Then other partners start to report the abusive treatment by the partner, i.e., the counterproductive effects of having this partner on the team. But the end result is that these "Diminishers" drive away talent. The best people in any field—the talented few who contribute the greatest value—simply don't have to put up with the misery perpetuated by a bad boss.[3] And they won't.

Just because a lawyer is a partner or is in some other leadership capacity does not necessarily mean that the lawyer has real leadership skills. You can advance your career and distinguish yourself from your colleagues by learning leadership skills—in particular, how to be a Multiplier instead of a Diminisher.

### *Learn to Have Difficult Conversations*

One of the most pervasive problems of dysfunctional organizations is that their leaders either avoid difficult conversations or have them badly. In this context, a "difficult" conversation is one in which the parties disagree about issues that have an emotional component to them and there is a great deal at stake. Ironically, although lawyers represent clients engaged in conflicts on a daily basis, when it comes to their own interpersonal conflicts, lawyers choose avoidance in most instances. An effective leader must learn how to have difficult conversations with subordinates, peers, and superiors in the chain of command. He must learn to tell the truth in a way that doesn't cause the other person either to flare up in anger or to shut down and stop talking altogether. If you can master this rare ability, you will become a highly respected leader.

In their book *Crucial Conversations: Tools for Talking When Stakes Are High*,[4] the business-consultant authors set forth a highly useful model to guide people in preparing for and engaging in these types of conversa-

---

[3] DANIEL GOLEMAN, RICHARD E. BOYATZIS & ANNIE MCKEE, PRIMAL LEADERSHIP: LEARNING TO LEAD WITH EMOTIONAL INTELLIGENCE 83 (Harvard Bus. Sch. Press 2004).

[4] KERRY PATTERSON, JOSEPH GRENNY, RON MCMILLAN & AL SWITZLER, CRUCIAL CONVERSATIONS: TOOLS FOR TALKING WHEN STAKES ARE HIGH (McGraw-Hill, 2d ed. 2012).

tions, which includes the following steps: examine your own motives, stay alert to signs of discomfort in others, create a safe environment for dialogue, recognize unfounded assumptions you may be making, tell the other person your assumptions and be willing to listen to their response. Below are brief discussions of each step, but *Crucial Conversations* elaborates on these and many more techniques that can be employed to conduct difficult conversation effectively.[5]

### Start with Heart

Before you engage in the conversation, think about what your motives and goals are for the conversation. What do you want to achieve? In many cases, you may be frustrated and angry with the other party. Try to recognize when you are motivated by these feelings, and separate those from the true objectives of the conversation. If you enter the conversation with nonemotional motives and can articulate an outcome that will provide something positive for both parties, it is much more likely to be successful.[6]

### Learn to Look

As you engage in the conversation, pay attention not only to the words being said but also to the conditions of the conversation. Is the other person giving signs that he doesn't feel comfortable? Does he feel attacked? In order to maintain dialogue in a difficult conversation, both people must feel safe. They must feel respected and believe that there is some mutual purpose to be gained from having and continuing the conversation. If these conditions don't exist, you may need to interrupt the content of the conversation and help the other person feel at ease.[7]

### Make It Safe

At the outset of your conversation, and whenever you see signs that the other person is shutting down or flaring up, create a safe environ-

---

[5] *Id.* at 9–17.
[6] *Id.* at 33–49.
[7] *Id.* at 51–72.

ment for the other person to express his views, which may be different from your own. The goal is to keep the dialogue going, with each person contributing the important ideas he has to share and explaining the rationale underlying his position, so that common ground can eventually be reached. Re-state the mutual purpose of the conversation (e.g., "we are both trying to make our department more successful") when necessary. Help the other person feel respected by not making personal attacks in the conversation, even acknowledge something you admire or respect about the other person. By paying attention to signals and re-establishing respect and mutual purpose, you will be able to maintain a dialogue that would otherwise break down.[8]

## Master Your Stories

Learn to recognize the stories you are telling yourself about the situation that is the subject of the conversation. Are you imputing motives to the other party that don't have a factual basis? Are you making assumptions about what the other person really wants? When you identify the stories you are telling yourself and separate them from the objective facts, you remove the emotional "triggers" from the conversation and open the opportunity for the other person to provide a different explanation from the one you assumed.[9]

## State Your Path and Explore Others' Paths

Once you understand the stories you are telling yourself and how they led you to the conclusions you have drawn, you can explain to the other person what you observed in terms of objective facts and state the conclusions you've drawn from your observations, giving the other person an opening to explain his perspective on the facts. It is critical in stating your path not to accuse or label the other person—just state what you've observed. For example, you might say, "I sent you an invitation to my presentation. You didn't respond, and you didn't attend the presentation. That caused me to conclude that you don't think my work or what

---

[8] *Id.* at 73–102.
[9] *Id.* at 103–130.

I have to say is important." The other person could then say, "I did get your invitation, but I had a conflict. I'm sorry—I should have RSVP'd. I do think your work is important." It is only after the facts and their different interpretations by the two parties are discussed that a mutual understanding can be reached.[10]

## Move to Action

As a mutual understanding is reached, it's important to establish a plan of action by agreeing who will do what, by when, after the conversation is over.[11]

Mastering the art of difficult conversations takes time and practice. You'll make mistakes as you try to implement the techniques described above. But over time, you will improve and have a valuable skill that distinguishes you from most other lawyers in your firm.

### *Take Leadership Roles*

## Serve on Firm Committees

Serving on one or more committees in the firm is a great way to use and develop your leadership skills. Depending on your particular interests and focus, you may choose recruiting, diversity, professional development, ethics, pro bono, or another committee in which to get involved. Serving on a committee may not increase your compensation directly; but even if it doesn't, you will reap rewards. Serving well on one of these committees—and eventually taking a leadership position—can enhance your value to the firm and the respect that you receive from your partners. As a committee leader, you will allow others in the firm to see more of your character, your dedication to the firm, and your ability to help others reach consensus.

When you take a role on a committee, take it seriously. Although client work is always a priority, committee work should never be

---

[10] *Id.* at 131–175.
[11] *Id.* at 177–187.

ignored. Serving poorly on a committee reflects badly on you and hurts your credibility within the firm. Accordingly, don't take on a committee role unless you are prepared to do the work it entails, to attend meetings, and to help the group advance its objectives.

### Volunteer in the Community

Giving back to the community is one of the most satisfying things you can do as a lawyer. There are hundreds of organizations in every community that would love to have your knowledge and background.

Decide which causes you are most passionate about. Once you've narrowed down the options, be strategic about your choice of organizations. There is nothing wrong with serving your "enlightened self-interest," that is, devoting yourself to a noble cause that may incidentally benefit you personally. Choose an organization that is aligned with your values and passions, and that will also expand your network in the direction you want to go, e.g., toward a particular industry or group of business leaders. Make sure that either (a) the organization's mission and the role you will play fit into your career goals, or (b) you care so much about the cause that it doesn't matter. If one or the other does not apply, you'll be miserable and wasting your time.

Once you start volunteering for an organization, you'll get to know it better. Spend a few years getting familiar with its mission, the way it raises money, the people involved, and the opportunities for growth. If you feel good about the organization, consider a board position when one becomes available, perhaps even chairing the board eventually. There are many leadership programs—through chambers of commerce, leadership organizations, and nonprofit cooperatives—geared toward preparing professionals to lead nonprofit organizations. Look into a program that will build your leadership skills and help you make valuable connections as well.

A word of caution, however: Set boundaries when you volunteer for nonprofits—they will want as much of your time as they can get. You may love the feeling of helping animals or impoverished children, but you have only so many hours in a day. Try to avoid getting caught up in too many organizations at once or taking on more assignments than you can effectively handle. You can lose track of your life if you're not careful. Make a pact with yourself about how many years you want to devote to a particular organization, and then stick with it.

### Learn to Run Great Meetings

When you are asked to chair a committee, board, or working group, you have a golden opportunity not only to help the firm or organization but also to build your prersonal brand and distinguish yourself as a leader. One way to do this is to run great meetings. Particularly on firm committees and in volunteer groups, poorly run meetings are the rule, not the exception. Time is wasted, and the group members develop biases against attending meetings or even having committees at all.

Run your meetings effectively, and you will not only accomplish more, you will increase the level of respect others have for you. The following are some ways to stand out by performing an administrative chore that everyone should be able to do, but few can do well:

(1) *Identify the purpose of the meeting.* When you set a meeting, decide what you want to accomplish and share that purpose with the people you are inviting to the meeting. Don't make the mistake of having a meeting just to hold a meeting or just because the group has historically met with a certain frequency. Know what result you want from the meeting.

(2) *Circulate an agenda before the meeting.* One of the best tools for running effective meetings is to prepare an agenda. This accomplishes three things: (1) it identifies the goal(s) of the meeting for all who will attend, (2) it helps the attendees to prepare for the meeting by thinking about the topics and what they will want to discuss, and (3) it helps the meeting to run smoothly by keeping its focus. An agenda need not be long or complicated, particularly if the topics are fairly straightforward

and the group has a limited purpose. How far in advance it should be circulated depends on the extent of preparation required of the participants: the more they will have to think about the topics, prepare for the meeting, and deliver some type of input at the meeting, the earlier you should circulate the agenda.

(3) *Prepare for the meeting.* One of the worst things that you can do to a group you are leading is to waste the group members' time, not only by having a meeting without a purpose, but also by arriving at the meeting unprepared. The process of preparing the agenda is good preparation for the meeting, but you should also schedule time on your calendar in advance of the meeting to walk though the agenda; think about what you are going to say and how the participants are likely to respond; and consider whether you need any visuals, diagrams, handouts, whiteboards, or flip charts in order to better explain important information. Think about ways you can help the group to understand the information you'll be discussing and to digest it as quickly as possible.

On the day of the meeting, have your assistant confirm details for the meeting: the location has been reserved, any necessary equipment or visuals will be ready, lunch or refreshments have been ordered, the room will be set up properly—anything that may affect the flow of the meeting. It may also be helpful to send a note to the meeting participants to remind them to attend and to complete any necessary preparation.

(4) *Start and end on time.* In almost any group, you will have participants who arrive on time and others who arrive late. If you show up late or wait until latecomers arrive before starting, you show disrespect for those who came on time and set a precedent for future meetings. It will be harder to get people there on time if they think you are going to waste the first several

minutes waiting for latecomers. Start on time and set that expectation for future meetings. You'll use the meeting time more efficiently, encourage members to arrive on time in the future to avoid missing important information, and show respect for the members who routinely arrive on time.

(5) *Don't recap for latecomers.* When you start on time and group members join the meeting late, avoid disruption if at all possible. Don't recap what's been said so far unless absolutely necessary. Giving a recap is the same as starting late, and potentially even more annoying. It wastes valuable time and tells the group members who were on time that their promptness was unnecessary. Let the latecomers get the information that was shared before they arrived from another group member after the meeting. They will learn that arriving late has consequences and that it is better to arrive on time.

(6) *Stick to the agenda.* Once the meeting starts, stick with the agenda to keep your meeting focused. Often, as a discussion progresses, group members wander off on tangents. As the facilitator of the meeting, it's your job to keep the group focused and on task. The agenda helps you steer the conversation back to the original purposes and to table newly-raised issues for future meetings.

While staying on track is important, however, it's also important not to rush through the agenda. Pay attention to the body language and words of the participants. Are they understanding the issues? Are they agreeing with the concepts? Spend more time on a topic if it will help the group members to better understand and buy into the decisions made.

If the meeting will last longer than an hour, be sure to provide periodic breaks. If you try to go much beyond an hour without providing a break, you will lose the attention of the group. Take a five- or ten-minute break, and then resume the meeting at the time you said you would. Failing to do so may cause you to lose participants, who will get frustrated wondering when the meeting is going to resume.

(7) *Use visuals.* Bring visuals to the meeting to help members follow a train of thought, a series of issues, or a previously created plan. If it will be a brainstorming meeting or group input will be sought, bring a whiteboard or flip chart so that emerging ideas can be recorded.

(8) *Draw people in.* It is also your job as facilitator to encourage participation and contribution by all group members at the meeting. This may mean asking for input from particular members who have been quiet during the meeting or gracefully putting an end to the comments of members who tend to monopolize meetings.

As noted in the discussion about sticking to the agenda, you should find the right balance between staying on track and not rushing. This is important to give members not only time to understand the issues, but also the chance to voice their opinions. Are you spending enough time on each topic so that people who have something to contribute have the opportunity to speak up? Don't be so focused on getting through the agenda that people feel rushed and unable to share their thoughts and ideas.

(9) *Keep the energy positive.* Depending on the type of group and its purpose, you are likely to have naysayers and wet blankets. Do everything you can to acknowledge the validity of the points they may be making, but at the same time note that other options may exist. Try not to get angry at or exasperated with naysayers; keep your optimism, and provide opportunities for the more optimistic members of your group to give voice to their suggestions and opinions. Don't let a meeting turn into a gripe session. When members of the group do feel compelled to gripe, press them for constructive solutions to the problems they have identified.

(10) *Always end with action steps.* Finally, make sure that shortly before the meeting ends, you recap any decisions made at the meeting, what the next steps will be, who is responsible for each follow-up step, and the deadline for the expected follow-up. In many cases, this deadline will be the next meeting. If possible, set the next meeting date before adjourning the current meeting. If that isn't possible, at least let the group members know generally when the next meeting will be, e.g., the last week of the following month, after a particular event has occurred, etc. Action steps are helpful not only for making sure that follow-up occurs, but also for highlighting the progress that was made at the meeting and confirming that the time was used for a productive purpose.

---

### Checklist for Running Better Meetings

1. Identify the purpose of the meeting.
2. Circulate an agenda in advance of the meeting.
3. Prepare for the meeting.
4. Start and end on time.
5. Don't recap information for latecomers.
6. Stick to the agenda.
7. Use visuals to illustrate important plans, points, or information.
8. Draw people in, i.e., encourage participation and discussion by everyone at the meeting.
9. Keep the energy positive.
10. Always end with action steps.

# CHAPTER FOURTEEN

# The Nitty-Gritty of Client and Practice Management

*"Life is not all fun and games."*

Although rainmaking may be the most celebrated partner contribution, an equally important area of contribution is practice management, i.e., managing client work in a way that maximizes its profitability and minimizes the firm's risk of not getting paid and/or facing a malpractice claim. Neglecting the fundamentals of sound practice management can undermine your practice altogether. Understanding the fundamental principles of profitable and ethical practice management is essential to building a successful career.

### Choose Your Clients Wisely

Generating new business isn't easy, so when you get a new client, the last thing you want to do is turn him away. But there are a few you *should* reject if you see the warning signs of a bad client. Particularly as a young partner just starting to build a book of business, it can be tempting to loosen your standards and take nearly any client who comes in the door. Resist this temptation. It's not worth the trouble later. Maintain your discipline in screening potential clients, and you'll avoid a host of difficult problems later on. Ignoring the warning signs can involve you in a situation that robs you of sleep, generates unpaid legal fees, and leads to malpractice claims. If you take a bad client because you didn't see the warning signs, you can still benefit by recognizing the signs as soon as possible so that you can reduce your risk.

Although by no means exhaustive, here is a list of five types of clients you should avoid if at all possible: the desperate, last-minute client; the serial client; the idealist; the habitual litigant; and the armchair quarterback.

## The Desperate, Last-Minute Client

This client contacts you, very excited about the help that you can provide. The only problem is that, due to circumstances that are no fault of his own, his lawsuit must be filed in two weeks, his deal must close tomorrow, his files must be turned over to a federal agency next Friday—you get the gist. You want to help him, and his goal seems achievable. Maybe you can be a hero. . . .

Be careful before jumping in to rescue such a client. Do you have time to do all that is necessary to competently represent this client? Can you get the information you need? Do you have the staffing? What obstacles might prevent you from accomplishing the goal? Some clients deliberately wait until relatively late to hire counsel, thinking they will save fees because the attorney will spend less time on the matter. Others simply drop the ball and want you to deal with the consequences. Still others actually have serious problems with their case or deal and think that by rushing you into it, you won't see how difficult it will be to complete. At best, you may complete the matter successfully but with more stress and risk than if you'd had the optimal amount of time to complete the representation. At worst, you can insert yourself into a no-win situation, get a bad result, and absorb blame for the failure in the form of unpaid fees or, worse, a malpractice claim.

## The Serial Client

The serial client knows all of the other lawyers in town, or at least the most prominent, who do the very kind of work that she is asking you to do. This client has talked to two or three other firms before coming to you and may even have retained one of them. But Lawyer X isn't doing a good enough job. The client wants to fire him and hire you. Be careful.

Before you take on this representation, do your best to find out what happened with the previous counsel. Make sure the client didn't withhold information, fail to pay, or harbor unrealistic expectations with the former counsel. There are times when a client legitimately may want to change lawyers and actually did hire someone less capable. But don't step in blindly, or you may be her next victim.

## The Idealist

The idealist comes in many packages: the client who thinks he'll win millions of dollars for a five-figure claim; the client who believes that justice is inexpensive and doesn't realize how much the matter is going to cost because he doesn't believe your estimate of the fees involved; or the client who is out to prove a point, even if it's not practical, and wants to pursue the case "on principle."

Before representing this type of client, determine whether you can establish realistic expectations on his part and educate him about what will really be involved in the case or deal. If you cannot, be prepared for a client who is perpetually dissatisfied.

## The Habitual Litigant

This client has been involved in a surprising number of lawsuits, and it's always the other party's fault. She could be a habitual plaintiff, constantly victimized by others and in need of compensation. She could be a habitual defendant, repeatedly attacked by "frivolous lawsuits."

Either way, be careful of the client who has a victim mentality. These people tend not to take responsibility for their own part in the disputes in their history; and if you don't win—or if you win but charge too much—she'll claim to be your victim, too.

## The Armchair Quarterback

Finally, we have the armchair quarterback client. This client comes in two forms: individual and corporate.

The individual armchair quarterback has actually done legal and factual research on his matter before consulting you, or he may have consulted a friend or relative who is a lawyer. Since he's done his homework, he thinks he knows what the outcome should be; and if you disagree, he may push back. He also may want a reduction in your fees, viewing himself as a team member who is saving you from the legwork he already did. This client will look over your shoulder and question your every move. Although it's good to have your client interested and involved in the matter, a client who tries to take too much control is likely to second-guess you later on, particularly if things don't go well.

The corporate armchair quarterback can be worse. Some corporate counsel are brilliant lawyers; others, not so much. If your corporate counsel is a great lawyer, you are way ahead in the game: she'll understand what you need from her and her team, make sure you get it, and have realistic expectations about the time and money it takes to do the job. If your client's counsel isn't a very good lawyer, that's not necessarily a bad thing if she defers to you and allows you to use your judgment. But if the client counsel is a micromanager, has a poor understanding of the law, and lacks sophistication in the type of case or deal for which you've been engaged—but thinks she knows it all—you may be in trouble. These armchair quarterbacks are often insecure, out to prove what they know and throw their weight around. If they defer to you, of course, they don't get to do this so they question your every move and pick apart your work, sometimes to make themselves look smarter.

You have little to gain with this kind of client. If you do well, the client counsel will take the credit. If the outcome is not so great, guess who will take the blame? Do your best to distinguish, as early as possible, those corporate counsel with whom you can work effectively from those you can't.

### Make Clear Who Is and Isn't Your Client

It may seem strange, but it is not always clear who is and isn't a client of a particular lawyer. Thus, it is important for lawyers to use nonengagement letters and engagement letters to clarify when they decline and accept prospective clients.

Many misunderstandings (and malpractice claims) arise when a prospective client consults a lawyer, and the lawyer—for whatever reason—declines the representation without clearly documenting that decision. After the consultation, a statute of limitations is blown or a deadline is missed, and the prospective client wants to blame you, claiming she didn't realize you weren't her lawyer.

The best way to avoid an unintentional representation is to consistently use nonengagement letters when you have had a conversation with a potential client whom you are not going to represent. This letter should (1) state clearly that the firm is not going to undertake the engagement or represent the client; (2) advise the client if there is a statute of limitations applicable to the claim discussed with you, though the letter should not cite a specific statute or purport to opine on the date it expires; (3) state the reason for not accepting the engagement, if appropriate; (4) disclaim any opinion on the merits of the matter and make clear that there was insufficient information exchanged on which specific advice could be given; and (5) advise the client to seek other counsel as soon as possible.

Just as important as nonengagement letters, engagement letters provide your best protection against misunderstandings with a client. Many states require such letters; and in many cases, it is difficult or impossible to collect disputed fees without one. Engagement letters define the scope of the representation so that the lawyer and the client are on the same page about what the lawyer *is* and *is not* expected to do for the client.

An effective engagement letter includes several elements. There are many optional provisions that can be included in an engagement letter, but the following are the provisions most essential to avoiding commonly encountered types of client misunderstandings:

- a clear identification of the client

- a description of the specific work that the lawyer has agreed to undertake (if there is a known or related matter that you are *not* handling, consider including a statement to that effect as well in order to avoid any confusion about the scope of representation)

- a clear description of the billing arrangement, including the method for computation (fixed versus hourly, etc.), the expected range of hourly billing rates, how often bills will be sent, when payment is expected, and what incidentals will be passed through directly versus what will be absorbed by the law firm (e.g., administrative expenses)

- a description of consequences of late payment, e.g., late fees or interest

- any special billing arrangements (and if multiple clients, which will be responsible for payment)

- any provisions required by your particular state's laws or ethics rules

- the name and contact information for the principal client contact

- a statement that the client should inform the lawyer immediately if he disagrees with anything in the letter

### Don't Go into Areas You Don't Know

When you agree to take on a client, make sure you either have the expertise necessary to do the work or have someone available in your firm who can provide that expertise, either directly to the client or through you. A high percentage of malpractice claims result from failure to know the law and, often related to that, missed deadlines. Particularly in difficult economic times, it can be tempting to take any kind of work that becomes available whether or not you know the area. Stay away from areas that you don't know.

This doesn't mean that you have to refuse a representation that may require some additional learning on your part, or refreshing yourself on something you haven't done in a while. Model Rule 1.1 of the *Model Rules of Professional Conduct* expressly states that "[a] lawyer may accept representation where the requisite level of competence can be achieved by reasonable preparation."[1] But if the area is fundamentally outside of your comfort zone, don't take on the representation.

---

[1] MODEL RULES OF PROF'L CONDUCT R. 1.1 (2012).

Instead, refer the business to a competent practitioner. Remember that these referrals are opportunities to build relationships with counsel in practice areas that are outside of your firm's expertise. Identify one or two practitioners you trust, and keep them in mind whenever you can make a referral in that area. Eventually, the other lawyer is likely to reciprocate.

### Set Realistic Expectations

The majority of client disputes can be prevented by managing the client's expectations effectively. When you begin an engagement, and throughout the entire course of the matter, it is critical to set realistic expectations for your client. Meet or beat all deadlines that you discuss with the client. Underpromise and overdeliver. The more the matter comports with what the client expected, the more satisfied the client is likely to be.

As discussed in chapter 11, good communication setting realistic expectations helps you build credibility and enhance the relationship. This process is also critical from a practice management standpoint, as realistic expectations reduce the likelihood of a fee dispute or malpractice claim.

### Communicate Frequently with the Client

A tremendous number of legal malpractice claims result from a lawyer's poor communication with a client in one way or another. Lawyers who don't communicate cause unnecessary anxiety for their clients, they cause themselves to be viewed less sympathetically, and they present the impression that they are indifferent to the client's matter. Avoid these problems. Stay in touch with your clients throughout your representation of them. Send them copies of all correspondence related to the matter, and inform them of all developments that may positively or negatively impact the outcome. If you are unsure, err on the side of overcommunicating.

One of the most frequent complaints that clients make about their lawyers is that they don't return their telephone calls and don't keep them apprised of what's going on in their matters. Return all phone calls and e-mails promptly, preferably within twenty-four hours. If you don't have time to return a call or respond to an e-mail, ask a colleague or assistant to contact the client. At the very least, let the client know that you received her inquiry and will respond by a certain date.

People are generally patient if they know when you will get back to them. In contrast, if they hear nothing, they tend to draw negative conclusions. They may ascribe significance to the delay; question your credibility; and, at worst, lose trust in you as their adviser and advocate. Clients who think that their lawyers don't care about them are more suspicious of them, and this skepticism can even affect whether they pay your bills. When something goes wrong, they are less likely to give you the benefit of the doubt and more likely to sue for malpractice. Stay in touch with your clients so that they know you care and are doing your best for them.

### Let the Client Know When the Representation Is Over

When you have concluded your work on a particular matter, send a closing letter so that the client knows that the representation is over. As provided in the comments to Model Rule 1.3 of the *Model Rules of Professional Conduct*, "[d]oubt about whether a client-lawyer relationship still exists should be clarified by the lawyer, preferably in writing, so that the client will not mistakenly suppose the lawyer is looking after the client's affairs when the lawyer has ceased to do so."[2] Again, it's a matter of managing expectations. Should a related matter arise in the future, you don't want your client to assume that you'll take care of it, or that you even know about it, if the matter you were engaged for is over.

### Be Meticulous About Billing and Timekeeping

One of the more arduous tasks in the practice of law is timekeeping. Although it is a task that many lawyers place at the bottom of the priority list and delay doing as much as possible, it is also one of the most critical to sustaining a profitable practice. Unfortunately, some of the

---

[2] *Id.* R. 1.3 (2012).

things that you have to do to be successful are not exciting. Writing down all of your time and tracking it in six-minute increments is not exciting. Writing descriptions of mundane work and trying to make them sound interesting is not exciting. Turning in your time every day is not exciting. However, you must discipline yourself to do it. You are doing yourself and your firm a disservice if you are not meticulous about billing and timekeeping because you will be cheating either the firm or the client.

There are some simple billing/timekeeping habits that can significantly increase the value of your work to the firm; and although you may already be aware of them, they bear repeating from time to time.

### Capture All of Your Time

Don't sell yourself short by "leaking" time, either by forgetting to record it or "self-editing" by consciously recording less time than you actually spent. As a newer lawyer, it will sometimes take longer to do particular assignments than you anticipated. Record all of your time anyway, and let the billing partner decide whether reductions are appropriate.

### Record Your Time Contemporaneously

Recording time contemporaneously is the best way to ensure that your time is both complete and accurate. Don't leave this task to the end of the day. Write down or type your entries as you do the tasks, and you won't have to worry about remembering it later. Even if you refer back to your e-mails at the end of the day, it is unlikely that you'll be able to recall and recreate every six-minute increment of the day.

### Submit or Enter Your Time Daily

In some billing systems, you may record your time and enter it in the billing system simultaneously. In others, it is a two-step process: you record your time by writing it (contemporaneously) on a notepad or an electronic document, and then enter or submit it to a billing system. If your system is not a one-step process, complete the second step by the end of each day before you go home.

## Describe Your Work in a Way That Makes the Client Want to Pay for It

When you write descriptions of the tasks you performed for a client, take pride in what you are writing and remember that this is one of the most important communications you will have with your client. You are explaining to the client why you deserve to be paid, and you do a great disservice to yourself and your firm if you do it in a way that is sloppy, careless, or uncommunicative.

In your descriptions, provide details about the issue you discussed, researched, analyzed, or resolved; describe specifically the people you met with, talked to, or wrote to; and explain the purpose of each task. If there was a particular benefit that arose from a task, include that in the description. It is better to err on the side of a long, detailed description of your work than to cut it short and say little.

This is important not only for communicating value to the client but also for malpractice purposes. The billing statements provide a record of the work you did. If you don't describe it specifically, you can't refer back and confirm what it was. In addition, detailed descriptions are important in the event the fees turn out to be recoverable and a court has to review the bills. A judge will carefully review whether the work done and the result achieved were worth the money that was charged. Protect yourself by creating a strong supporting document about the services you provide to your clients.

## Proofread Draft Bills Carefully

Lawyers dislike reviewing draft bills—whether labeled prebills, pro formas, or some other term—almost as much as they dislike the chore of timekeeping. But it is essential. Just as it is important to write clear, carefully crafted work descriptions, it's important to proofread and edit prebills so that clients don't receive sloppy bills.

# CHAPTER FIFTEEN

# Be a Good Partner: Ask Not What Your Firm Can Do for You

*A Lion used to prowl about a field in which Four Oxen used to dwell. Many a time he tried to attack them; but whenever he came near they turned their tails to one another, so that whichever way he approached them he was met by the horns of one of them. At last, however, they fell a-quarrelling among themselves, and each went off to pasture alone in a separate corner of the field. Then the Lion attacked them one by one and soon made an end of all four.*

*United we stand, divided we fall.*

*—Aesop[1]*

There are pros and cons to having partners. On the plus side, you have people to share the risk when your practice isn't going so well, to chip in and help pay for administrative resources, and to bounce ideas off of and to use as a resource when a client has a question you can't answer or needs a kind of help that you can't provide. On the minus side, you have to share the rewards when your practice is doing well (and your partners' practices may not be doing well), negotiate with others on how to allocate resources and listen to others' two cents when you don't necessarily want to hear it. People join firms when they get tired of handling all of the administrative aspects of running a law firm and want to col-

---

[1] Aesop, *The Four Oxen and the Lion*, in AESOP'S FABLES, http://www.aesopfables.com/cgi/aesop1.cgi?sel&The FourOxenandtheLion (last visited Nov. 25, 2012).

laborate; partners leave firms when they get tired of perceived unfairness or imbalance of power or compensation.

If you decide you want to go the partner route, you should understand that practicing in a firm means more than just sharing administrative resources and splitting profits. Given the degree of autonomy and independence that lawyers cherish and the focus of legal journals and industry publications on the practice of law as a business rather than a profession, partners often forget that they must stick together to sustain a successful firm. Whether a lawyer has two partners or two hundred, the ability to keep the firm's best interests in mind and think beyond the individual benefit is crucial to the survival of the firm. As an associate, it's important to prepare yourself for this role and recognize the responsibilities that go with it.

### Bring in Business

Perhaps the most obvious contribution that a partner is expected to make is to bring in business. Occasionally, a firm may make someone a partner who is not a good business generator but fills a valuable role in servicing other partners' clients. However, for the most part, a partner is expected to bring in business that will not only keep the partner busy but will keep associates and potentially paralegals busy as well. As a rule of thumb, many firms expect a partner to bring in enough business to generate revenues equivalent to three times the partner's salary each year.

It's not only the quantity of clients that matters—it's the quality as well. Partners have to be able to trust that the others will not knowingly bring in clients who are unlikely to pay, who are likely to sue, or who seek a relationship that is incompatible with the business objectives of the firm.

### Cross-Sell

In firms that have lawyers in a variety of practice areas, partners are typically expected to recommend their partners to their own clients when the clients have needs in their partners' areas of specialty. For example, if you are a real estate lawyer and your client identifies a tax problem, you should involve a partner who is a tax specialist. If you are a corporate lawyer and your client needs to file a collection lawsuit, you should refer the client to a litigation partner. Some partners are reluctant to do this, either because they made such a referral in the past and it went badly or because they are possessive of their clients and afraid other partners will build relationships with them. This is bad for a firm and breeds an "eat what you kill" mentality.

There are a number of adverse consequences to not sharing clients with your partners. For example, if you try to serve a client in a practice area outside of your area of expertise, you may make costly mistakes or run into malpractice issues. If you refuse to allow other partners to have contact with your clients, you may limit the amount of business you can generate to the amount you can directly supervise. You miss out on the opportunity to create a reciprocal relationship that may lead to business for you someday. You also may be denying a less experienced lawyer the opportunity to develop client relationship skills. None of these outcomes are good for the firm.

### Protect the Firm's Assets

Although the topic is not often discussed, partners owe fiduciary duties to each other. These include duties of good faith, care, and loyalty to the firm and fellow partners. One aspect of fiduciary duty is to be conscious when you are using firm assets, not waste or squander them. When traveling, be mindful of the firm's travel policy and don't spend exorbitant amounts. If given a budget, stay within it. If you are given the choice between an expensive boondoggle and a local educational conference with the same quality of content, attend the local conference. Hundreds of small decisions must be made over the course of the year, and you'll need to make these in a way that respects the co-ownership rights of your partners.

One asset that partners are sometimes careless about is their billable time. It will be your fiduciary duty as a partner to record all of the time you spend working on matters for the firm's clients, to capture it effectively, and to submit it—whether directly into a billing system or to an administrative assistant who will enter it—promptly. Failing to record your time contemporaneously can cause you to lose it, effectively squandering an asset of the firm.

Along the same lines, get the firm's permission before providing legal services to a nonfirm client, whether it is a friend, a family member, or a pro bono client. Doing work for nonpaying clients is effectively giving away some of the firm's inventory of billable time. Although it's a generally accepted practice in most firms, it should always be done with full disclosure to the firm and after a conflicts check, just as you would do with any paying client matter.

### *Promote Compliance with the* Model Rules of Professional Conduct

Particularly as firms grow larger and partners divide into specializations, many forget that they are responsible for ensuring ethical conduct throughout the firm. Under Model Rule 5.1(a) of the *Model Rules of Professional Conduct,* a partner in a law firm "shall make reasonable efforts to ensure that the firm has in effect measures giving reasonable assurance that all lawyers in the firm conform to the Rules of Professional Conduct."[2] Your firm may have an ethics committee that administers rules and policies for complying with this obligation. Even so, you are not absolved of personal responsibility for ensuring ethical conduct. Provide input to your ethics committee as you see potential problems, be mindful of the way you run your own practice, and teach the lawyers who work for you to practice ethically.

### *Enhance the Firm's Reputation*

When you interact with other counsel, courts, the media, or any businessperson outside of your firm, remember that your actions speak not only for yourself but also for your firm. Make decisions in your interactions that will enhance the firm's reputation rather than compromising it.

---

[2] MODEL RULES OF PROF'L CONDUCT R. 5.1(a) (2012).

### Support Important Initiatives and Decisions

As a co-owner of the firm, you are expected to support the decisions of the firm's management. You may not agree with all of them, but it's important that you present a unified front to the staff and associates when the firm makes a decision. This may include unpopular decisions such as salary freezes, reductions in holidays or benefits, or cuts in certain expenses. Similar to a political party, there may be much debate while selecting a candidate or making a decision; but once the decision is made, everyone needs to stand behind it because disagreement undermines the credibility of the decision and fosters division among the ranks.

Managing partners vary in their styles of leadership, and this can affect the degree to which the partners buy into particular decisions. Some firms adopt a democratic style of leadership. This style emphasizes allowing many different partners to provide input on important decisions. It is a difficult style to maintain at times because the decision-making process can get bogged down and take a long time while various partners debate the pros and cons. Once a decision is reached, however, it tends to have great support and buy-in because the partners had a say in it. In contrast, some leaders use an autocratic, or "benevolent dictator," form of leadership. Under this style, decisions are often made unilaterally by the managing partner. This can be a very efficient way to run a firm if the managing partner is trusted by his colleagues and generally treats everyone fairly. If the managing partner is not trusted and exercises an authoritative style, however, it can lead to resentment among those who disagree and don't feel that they were given the opportunity to provide input to which they were entitled.

### Participate in Management

Partners also have a duty to participate in the management of the firm. This can be accomplished through various means and may include everything from following administrative guidelines for submitting expenses to serving on firm committees to chairing a practice group.

Law firms vary in the way they manage themselves, from having no professional management, and entirely managing themselves with lawyers, to having a larger staff and reducing the time that lawyers have to spend on management activities. Even firms with large staffs, however, require attorney participation in management to establish policies, make important decisions, and perpetuate the firm's culture and values.

Take your turn and serve on your firm's committees for—or as the partner in charge of—activities such as recruiting, professional development, diversity, and pro bono service. Take your role seriously, particularly if you are the chair of a committee. Your reputation may be affected if you neglect to hold meetings, resolve issues, and make decisions. Although it's easy for the lawyer in this role to de-prioritize the work required because it's not for a paying client, the fact is that the way you manage your role affects the way that others (partners, associates, and staff) perceive you. Slacking off in a committee role may eliminate you as a candidate for higher leadership positions in the firm later on.

Rather than viewing a committee position as a burden, think of the opportunities that such a position presents. Committee positions can provide an opportunity to build relationships with key players within your firm, particularly those with whom you don't typically work in your practice group. They also give you the opportunity to use your skills and abilities in a new way; for example, your understanding of human nature can be valuable in a recruiting committee role. They also allow you to learn more about the management of a law firm, and your firm in particular. It's easy to criticize management when you've never had to serve in a management role or solve the kinds of problems that arise in any organization. Taking these roles will give you a greater appreciation for all of the non-legal skills and knowledge that are necessary to make a firm run successfully.

# CHAPTER SIXTEEN

# Character: Integrity, Civility, and Class

*The Boy Who Cried Wolf*

*There once was a shepherd boy who was bored as he sat on the hillside watching the village sheep. To amuse himself he took a great breath and sang out, "Wolf! Wolf! The Wolf is chasing the sheep!" The villagers came running up the hill to help the boy drive the wolf away. But when they arrived at the top of the hill, they found no wolf. The boy laughed at the sight of their angry faces. "Don't cry 'wolf', shepherd boy," said the villagers, "when there's no wolf!" They went grumbling back down the hill.*

*Later, the boy sang out again, "Wolf! Wolf! The wolf is chasing the sheep!" To his naughty delight, he watched the villagers run up the hill to help him drive the wolf away. When the villagers saw no wolf they sternly said, "Save your frightened song for when there is really something wrong! Don't cry 'wolf' when there is NO wolf!" But the boy just grinned and watched them go grumbling down the hill once more. Later, he saw a REAL wolf prowling about his flock. Alarmed, he leaped to his feet and sang out as loudly as he could, "Wolf! Wolf!"*

*But the villagers thought he was trying to fool them again, and so they didn't come. At sunset, everyone wondered why the shepherd boy hadn't returned to the village with their sheep. They went up the hill to find the boy. They found him weeping. "There really was a wolf here! The flock has scattered! I cried out, "Wolf!" Why didn't you come?"*

*An old man tried to comfort the boy as they walked back to the village. "We'll help you look for the lost sheep in the morning," he said, putting his arm around the youth, "Nobody believes a liar . . . even when he is telling the truth!"*

Once upon a time, you were a bright-eyed law school graduate with dreams of doing good deeds in the world, fully intending to become an ethical, honorable lawyer. Some lawyers are able to preserve that attitude throughout their careers. Others become jaded. Others have occasional lapses. There are times in your career when you may be tempted to sacrifice your character, i.e., your integrity, your civility, and your class. However, as one senior associate observed, "your reputation is the single most valuable asset you have. It only takes one bad act to ruin it." When temptation arises, step away from the moment and look at the bigger picture. Imagine yourself looking back on your career on the day you retire. Do you want to have any regrets? Envision the way you want your colleagues to remember you and how you would want them to describe your professionalism to your children. That will help you keep things in perspective and avoid taking the wrong path.

### *Integrity: Take the High Road*

You may see other lawyers who act in a dishonest or unethical way yet appear to be successful (i.e., make a lot of money). Don't follow their example. Remember that behind the scenes, in ways you may know nothing about, they are paying a price for their lack of integrity.

### Credibility

Clients hire lawyers to analyze, advise, strategize, advocate, mediate, transact, and engage in myriad other activities to accomplish their objectives. Although the services lawyers provide occupy a broad spectrum, nearly all of them have one thing in common: a lawyer can't perform them, or at least perform them well, without credibility. Without credibility, a lawyer can't provide analyses that clients will accept or advice that clients will follow; without credibility, a lawyer can't persuade a decision maker to reach a particular conclusion; and without credibility, a lawyer can't negotiate effectively with opposing counsel. In short, you have little to offer a client if your word means nothing.

## Ethics

Lawyers encounter ethical issues frequently, whether they recognize them or not. Take the time to familiarize yourself with the rules. When in doubt about what to do, ask for advice.

Some of the most common ethical pitfalls include the following:

- *You make a mistake in representing a client—you overlooked some important information, made a wrong assumption, or accidentally disclosed confidential information to the other side—and want to cover it up.* Don't do this. When considering how to handle the situation, don't rely solely on your own judgment as you may not be in the best position to evaluate the situation objectively. Go tell an ethics committee member or a senior partner whom you trust. In many cases, the mistake may be easier to correct than you think. At the very least, you and your firm can start working to rectify it with the client. If you cover it up, you risk exacerbating the situation, creating a more serious malpractice claim and severely damaging your credibility. All lawyers make mistakes. Your partners will stand behind you if they can trust you to own up and admit yours when you make them.

- *You are short on meeting your billable-hour requirement for a given year and are tempted to pad your time.* Don't. Do everything you can to find legitimate billable work if your hours are light. Look for opportunities to do pro bono work, if your firm gives billable credit for it. After you've done that, you've done all you can. Accept that you may not get a bonus or be recognized as having a great year, and take comfort in the fact that your integrity is intact.

- *You are working on a great, sexy case for a high-profile client and want to impress people by telling them about it.* Be careful. Obviously, you can't repeat what the client has told you or advice you have given because attorney-client privilege protects these communications. But your duty to protect client confidentiality goes much further than the privilege rules. Even if what you are disclosing can be found somewhere in a "public document" on file with the court or county clerks office, you may still breach your duty of confidentiality by talking about it if it's something the client does not want publicized. In fact, the mere fact that you are representing a particular client is generally confidential unless that client has chosen to disclose it publicly. Read Model Rule 1.6 of the *Model Rules of Professional Conduct* (or your state's equivalent rule) thoroughly, and err on the side of not discussing client matters.[1] Remember that once you release information, you can never take it back.

- *You are working with a senior lawyer who wants to take a course of action that doesn't sound right to you.* Don't blindly follow along. You cannot assume that if a partner made the decision, you will be insulated from responsibility for the violation. Do some research, on your own time if you must, to try and confirm whether the course of action is ethical. Raise your concerns to the senior lawyer. If the senior lawyer continues to insist on a course of action that you feel is unprofessional or unethical, talk to another partner whom you trust. It may be awkward and it may cause the partner to be angry, but it's better to try and protect yourself and the firm than stay silent because you're afraid of upsetting a partner.

### Be Civil and Courteous to Other Lawyers

It should go without saying: be civil and courteous to other lawyers, including opposing counsel. Most young lawyers intuitively know this, and they enter the profession with the best of intentions. Then something happens, usually some combination of witnessing unprofessional

---

[1] MODEL RULES OF PROF'L CONDUCT R. 1.6 (2012).

behavior by their senior colleagues and getting frustrated with an un-cooperative opposing counsel over a particular communication or series of interactions. The young lawyer may be tempted to emulate more experienced lawyers, who should know better but still act unprofession-ally by, for example, "retrading" in negotiations, refusing to make insignificant concessions (e.g., agreeing to an extension of time), filing unfounded motions in court, making unfounded assertions in a negoti-ation, raising their voice in a disagreement, slamming down the phone, making personal attacks on opposing counsel, and even in some cases misrepresenting the facts.

Many lawyers who act this way will say that they are being "zealous advocates," which they claim is not only permitted but required for com-petency under the ethical rules. However, many are not aware that Canon 7 of the *Model Code of Professional Responsibility*, which stated that "[a] lawyer shall represent a client zealously within the bounds of the law,"[2] has been replaced by ABA Model Rule 1.3 of the *Model Rules of Professional Conduct*, which states that "[a] lawyer shall act with rea-sonable diligence and promptness in representing a client."[3] This change was designed specifically to remove any suggestion that "reasonable dili-gence" includes offensive tactics or uncivil behavior. The comment makes clear that while a lawyer must act with commitment and dedica-tion to the interests of the client, and "with zeal in advocacy on the clients behalf," a lawyer is not bound to press every advantage that might be realized for a client.

Some unprofessional lawyers truly believe that they are more effec-tive when they act in an overly aggressive manner because, in the short term, they may win some small advantage (e.g., a concession in a nego-tiation or a decision in court, often obtained by simply wearing down the other side). In the long run, however, these tactics will get you nowhere at best and damage your reputation at worst. Gaining a reputation for incivility will cost you. There will be lawyers who won't want to negoti-

---

[2] MODEL CODE OF PROF'L RESPONSIBILITY Canon 7 (2012).
[3] MODEL RULES OF PROF'L CONDUCT R. 1.3(a) (1983).

ate with you, settlements you won't be able to obtain for your clients, and concessions that others will refuse to give you because you denied the same to them. Noted one senior associate:

> "You lose credibility by being nasty. Know the difference between being aggressive and being rude or unprofessional. Use the style that works for you; don't be aggressive if that's not your style. You can be very effective with a soft approach if you are firm in seeking your objectives and have a complete mastery of the facts."

### Show Class with Your Colleagues

Beyond the purview of both the rules of ethics and the customs of professionalism, consider the importance of showing class when dealing with your colleagues. The notion of "class" has no single definition, but you're likely to recognize it when you see it. It's when you do something you don't have to do because it's particularly considerate or just the right thing to do.

A "class act" is someone who can shake hands and congratulate opposing counsel—perhaps even sending a note—after losing a trial to them, someone who remembers his secretary's birthday, someone who takes significant time to help a junior lawyer understand how to write a particular document even when he can't bill for the time, someone who is secure enough in his own capabilities to grant client access to team members and fellow partners, and someone who doesn't complain if on a rare occasion someone else gets credit for his work but who conspicuously gives credit to his team when a major accomplishment is achieved.

Class is also embodied by a person who gives two or more weeks' notice, even if he is eager to start a new job, and passes on critical information to the team members who will take over his matters. And, most of all, class is demonstrated by a lawyer who resists the temptation to disparage the firm as he leaves it—even if he was asked to leave and even if he feels wronged.

In short, you display class anytime you contribute to others in a positive way without obligation and without expecting anything in return. Like karma, class will come back to you if you send it around.

### Don't Let a Client Ruin Your Reputation

Some lawyers aren't inclined to act unprofessionally in general but become unprofessional in representing a particular client. Be careful of clients over whom you have little control. Although some clients will follow all of the advice that you give them and others will follow most of it, a few will want you to pursue their goals in unethical or unprofessional ways. In these instances, you must be firm. Either persuade the client to follow an up-and-up approach, or withdraw from representing them. Working for too many of these kinds of clients (and in some cases, one can be too many) can jeopardize your reputation and impair your effectiveness as a lawyer.

Consider the following real-life example, in which a firm lost the respect—and business—of another firm because it acted unprofessionally and unethically in its representation of a certain client.

> I had an opposing counsel who had been very adversarial. Throughout a very contentious piece of real estate litigation, he filed an excessive number of motions, was uncooperative in many ways, and put our client to a lot of expense. At one point early in the case, we had discussed settlement, but our clients were very far apart. A couple of months before trial, opposing counsel wanted to schedule a settlement conference. I didn't think it was a good idea. I told him that I didn't want to waste my client's time or money, and based on what had transpired to that point, it was going to be a waste of time. He pushed the point in a couple of follow up conversations. I told him I wouldn't agree to it unless he would make sure to have a client representative present whowould have real authority to move from the positions we last discussed. He promised that would be the case.
>
> I persuaded my client to agree to the settlement conference, though it wasn't easy. worked with our appraiser to prepare a summary of his testimony, to provide to the mediator. I forced my client to come up with a range

of settlement numbers he could live with. Despite opposing counsel's representations to me, it was apparent they had no intent of settling. We could barely agree on a single point. We spent most of the day arguing the facts of the case, with various breakout sessions. Eventually, the opposing side informed us that they were not prepared to make a settlement offer. I was livid. The law firm representing the opposing landowner has worked with us as co-counsel in the past, and we've referred clients to them when we had conflicts. Apparently, they just wanted to get a preview of how we would present our case at trial, and weren't serious about settling at all. I do not intend to send them future work, and if they're ever on the other side of us on a case, we won't rely on a word they say.

CHAPTER SEVENTEEN

# The Big Picture

*"The Dog and the Shadow"*

*It happened that a Dog had got a piece of meat and was carrying it home in his mouth to eat it in peace. Now on his way home he had to cross a plank lying across a running brook. As he crossed, he looked down and saw his own shadow reflected in the water beneath. Thinking it was another dog with another piece of meat, he made up his mind to have that also. So he made a snap at the shadow in the water, but as he opened his mouth the piece of meat fell out, dropped into the water and was never seen more.*

*"BEWARE LEST YOU LOSE THE SUBSTANCE BY GRASPING AT THE SHADOW."*

—*Aesop's Fables*

What this book is really about is "All the Other Stuff"—the capabilities you need beyond legal skills in order to build a successful career. A surprising number of associates overlook these capabilities, and a surprising number of law firms fail to emphasize them until too late in their associates' careers. Although new lawyers should focus their first two or three years on learning the practice and honing core legal skills, they can accelerate their long-term success if they start learning All the Other Stuff at the late-junior to early-midlevel stage of their careers.

## Take a Long-Term View of Your Career

If you're at the midlevel stage, ready to start learning these additional skills, you may be thinking, "This is too much work. I'm already billing eighteen or nineteen hundred hours per year. On top of that, you're suggesting I spend hundreds of additional hours each year on All the Other Stuff, too?"

Yes. Unfortunately, many associates don't realize that, particularly in the early years of their careers, the billable-hour number is *not* the total contribution expected by most firms, nor is it the total amount of time necessary to build a solid career foundation. Billable work is just one component, albeit the lion's share, of the time commitment that you must make to your career. In addition to whatever billable-hour goals you set for yourself, you should plan to spend another four hundred hours or so on All the Other Stuff.[1]

"But I'm not sure I want to be a partner," you may say. "So why should I even worry about All the Other Stuff?"

Because it's All the Other Stuff that will differentiate you from other lawyers after the first three to four years of your career. And it's All the Other Stuff that will determine whether you ultimately end up as a service partner or staff attorney rather than a self-sustaining partner or sole practitioner. In other words, it's All the Other Stuff that, if you have it, will allow you the most freedom, independence, and control over your career.

## Hypotheticals

Consider Cyrus, a hypothetical associate who works studiously on documents and writes brilliant briefs but hasn't developed any people skills. After Cyrus makes partner, how many clients will he develop? Without the ability to develop business or strong relationships through-out the firm that generate internal work for him, how highly will he be valued by the firm? The harsh reality is that the firm can almost always go out and hire another brilliant law school graduate who will eventually draft documents or write briefs as well as Cyrus can.

---

[1] *See, e.g.*, Am. Bar Ass'n, ABA Commission on Billable Hours Report 50 (Aug. 2002) (describing a model "diet" of 1,900 hours per year of billable client work, 100 hours of pro bono work, 100 hours of service to the firm, 75 hours of client development, 75 hours of training and professional development, and 50 hours of service to the profession).

Now consider Jason, a hypothetical associate who not only produces high quality work but goes out of his way to build relationships with existing clients; keeps his practice profitable by meticulously recording his time and describing its value; gains visibility in the community by serving on nonprofit boards; and maintains a network of professional peers that he can go to for advice, support, and eventually, business.

How easy is Jason to replace versus Cyrus? Exactly. The more you develop capabilities in All the Other Stuff in addition to legal skills, the more valued you will be by your firm and the closer you will come to reaching "indispensable" status.

## "Indispensable" Status

What is the value of "indispensable" status? Priceless. "The best advice I've ever received, and in turn given to new lawyers," said Miles Cortez, a corporate executive and former senior partner, "is the following: Render yourself invaluable. Get so good at lawyering that the thought of losing you will terrorize your clients or your employer. It's the key to economic self-sufficiency."[2]

If you have "indispensable" status, you have freedom. Do you want to pursue long-term partnership with your current firm? Great—then you have the freedom to stay. You're likely to be highly compensated, given a variety of important roles, and have increasing ability to control your schedule by delegating work as you rise in seniority. You'll also attract mentors more readily than other associates. Would you like to change firms? Great—then you have the freedom to go. If you're like Jason, you'll be an attractive lateral candidate and will have many employment opportunities. Would you like to go solo? Great—then you have the freedom to do so. If you're like Jason, you can do it because you have a wide range of skills and are much better equipped to start your own practice.

Gaining "indispensable" status also means a greater ability to balance life and work in the long run. Although in the early years investing

---

[2] Interview with Miles Cortez, Corporate Counsel, Aimco, in Denver, Colo.

twenty-three hundred hours per year in your career may feel intense, it's an investment that will pay off in the future if it provides you with more power to choose the firm you work for, the clients you serve, the type of practice you run, and the people who work on your team. In today's world, the "immediate gratification" dynamic is everywhere. You can distinguish yourself by making sacrifices early in your career in order to have more choices and control later on.

Even as a senior associate, your investment may start to pay off and give you leverage to ask for what you want. For example, most firms, even very progressive ones, don't allow associates to work part-time (unless they are on a nonpartnership track or are hired on a contract basis). But after working to build both solid legal skills and a promising start on All the Other Stuff, an associate who gains "indispensable" status has a much better chance of successfully negotiating a flexible or reduced-hour arrangement.

### Keep It All in Perspective

Although a successful legal career is worth striving for and working hard for, you also have to keep it in perspective. It's not everything. Don't take it so seriously that you sacrifice your health, your family relationships, or your friends in the process. You'll need them as you encounter the inevitable bumps that punctuate every lawyer's career.

As you get more comfortable balancing All the Other Stuff with your legal work and personal life, you'll find that there are often ways to kill multiple birds with one stone. For example, you may be able to bring your significant other to a charity dinner and have both a "date" and a networking opportunity. You'll also find, in many cases, that your clients become your friends and vice versa. When that's the case, your "client entertainment" time becomes enjoyable personal time as well. Pro bono work may also provide a venue for combining a personal passion with your professional talent.

If you have a significant other, make sure that he or she is on the same page regarding the time that you need to commit to your career. Communicate openly about your goals and intentions and what it will

take to get there. Building a legal career is difficult enough without conflict at home. Establish priorities and realize that, at different career
stages, priorities may need to shift from time to time.

Despite the frustrations and challenges of being a lawyer, try to keep
things in perspective. Cultivate a sense of gratitude and humility. "The
more I can separate myself from the feeling that I'm 'special' or more
important than others because I'm a lawyer, the more satisfying my work
is," said one senior associate, "[and] the better I can balance my life and
go home at the end of the day. It helps to keep me from blowing both
the successes and failures out of proportion." Remember that you are
fortunate to have a career that pays relatively well, provides intellectual
stimulation, and allows you to help people with some of their most challenging problems.

When you have a bad day, remember that things will get better.
When you have a good day, enjoy it. When you win a big victory or close
a big deal, celebrate it. And if your career is stalling, assess yourself, step
up, and work on All the Other Stuff.

# Resources

## *Self-Assessment*

Tom Rath, STRENGTHSFINDER 2.0 (2007)

## *Self-Promotion and Visibility*

Peggy Klaus, BRAG! THE ART OF TOOTING YOUR OWN HORN WITHOUT BLOWING IT (2003)

## *Leadership*

Daniel Goleman, Richard E. Boyatzis & Annie McKee, PRIMAL LEADERSHIP: LEARNING TO LEAD WITH EMOTIONAL INTELLIGENCE (Harvard Bus. Sch. Press, 2004)

David H. Maister, ARE LAW FIRMS MANAGEABLE?, AM. LAW. (2006)

Patrick J. McKenna & David H. Maister, FIRST AMONG EQUALS (2005)

Kerry Patterson, Joseph Grenny, Ron McMillan & Al Switzler, CRUCIAL CONVERSATIONS: TOOLS FOR TALKING WHEN STAKES ARE HIGH (McGraw-Hill, 2d ed., 2012)

Liz Wiseman & Greg McKeown, MULTIPLIERS: HOW THE BEST LEADERS MAKE EVERYONE SMARTER (2010)

## *Client Relationships*

ATTORNEY AT WORK, www.attorneyatwork.com (last visited Nov. 26, 2012)

Jay G. Foonberg, HOW TO START AND BUILD A LAW PRACTICE, 5th ed. (American Bar Association, 2004)

Malcolm Gladwell, BLINK: THE POWER OF THINKING WITHOUT THINKING (Little, Brown, 2005)

Daniel Goleman, EMOTIONAL INTELLIGENCE: WHY IT CAN MATTER MORE THAN IQ (TalentSmart, 2007)

David H. Maister, ADVICE TO A YOUNG PROFESSIONAL 1 (2005), *available at* davidmaister.com/pdf/SomeAdvicetoaYoungProfessional 20912.pdf

David H. Maister, Charles H. Green & Robert M. Galford, THE TRUSTED ADVISOR (Free Press, 2000)

Theda Snyder, WOMEN RAINMAKERS' BEST MARKETING TIPS (3d ed., 2011)

### Legal Career Satisfaction

Nancy Levit & Douglas O. Linder, THE HAPPY LAWYER: MAKING A GOOD LIFE IN THE LAW (2010)

Patrick J. Schiltz, ON BEING A HAPPY, HEALTHY, AND ETHICAL MEMBER OF AN UNHAPPY, UNHEALTHY, AND UNETHICAL PROFESSION, 52 VAND. L. REV. 871 (1999)

Anne-Marie Slaughter, WHY WOMEN STILL CAN'T HAVE IT ALL, ATLANTIC MAG. (July/Aug. 2012).

# Index